LIBERATING THEORY

LIBERATING THEORY

By

Michael Albert
Leslie Cagan
Noam Chomsky
Robin Hahnel
Mel King
Lydia Sargent
Holly Sklar

SOUTH END PRESS

Editing, typesetting, and layout by South End Press
Charts and graphs by Elizabeth Stahl
Cover design by Elizabeth Stahl

Library of Congress Cataloging-in-Publication Data

Liberating theory.

    1. Social sciences--Methodology. 2. United States--Social conditions--1945-   United States--Politics and government--1945-   4. United States--Economic conditions--1945-   . I. Albert, Michael, 1947-   . II Title.
H61.L514   1986   306'.0973   86-13032
ISBN 0-89608-307-1
ISBN 0-89608-306-3 (pbk.)   20/30

www.southendpress.org
South End Press, 7 Brookline Street, #1, Cambridge, MA 02139-4146

07 06 05 04 03 02   7 8 9 10 11 12

ACKNOWLEDGEMENTS

We wish to thank the extended network of people who influenced this project through writing, discussion and, in some cases, lengthy interviews: Peter Bohmer, Michael Bronski, Sandy Carter, Ward Churchill, Marilyn Clement, David Dellinger, Ros Everdell, Jeanne Gallo, Dick Greenwood, Todd Jailer, Barbara Joseph, Joyce King, Winona LaDuke, Antonia Pantoja, Cynthia Peters, Helen Rodriguez, Rosaria Salerno, John Schall, Juliet Schor, Stephen Shalom, Howard Stanback, Jack Tchen, and Leah Wise. Special thanks to Elizabeth Stahl for her skillful production work.

Selected Titles of Interest

Michael Albert: *Stop the Killing Train: Radical Visions for Radical Change; Looking Forward* and *Unorthodox Marxism* with Robin Hahnel; and *Beyond Survival* with David Dellinger.

Leslie Cagan: "Feminism and Militarism" in *Beyond Survival*; "Something New Emerges: The Growth of a Socialist Feminist" in *They Should Have Served That Cup of Coffee*.

Noam Chomsky: *Year 501: The Conquest Continues, Rethinking Camelot, Necessary Illusions,* and *On Power and Ideology*.

Robin Hahnel: *Looking Forward, Unorthodox Marxism, Marxism and Socialist Theory,* and *Socialism Today and Tomorrow*, all with Michael Albert.

Mel King: *Chain of Change; From Access to Power: Black Politics and Power,* with James Jennings.

Lydia Sargent: *Women and Revolution; Playbook,* with Maxine Klein and Howard Zinn.

Holly Sklar: *Streets of Hope: The Fall and Rise of an Urban Neighborhood,* with Peter Medoff; *Trilateralism: The Trilateral Commission and Elite Planning for World Management; Poverty in the American Dream,* with Karin Stallard and Barbara Ehrenreich.

About The Authors

Michael Albert edits *Z Magazine*. He has previously been involved in diverse movements and organizations concerning anti-war, community, and socialist organizing.

Leslie Cagan is an organizer who has been involved in hundreds of movement events and projects. She is currently working in the Cuba solidarity movement.

Noam Chomsky is a professor of linguistics at MIT in Cambridge, MA and has been a tireless critic of U.S. foreign policy and historian of its logic and abuses. He has championed human rights all over the world and has participated in diverse struggles for social change and against U.S. imperialism.

Robin Hahnel is a professor of economics at American University in Washington D.C. and a participant in diverse anti-war, community, socialist, and anti-interventionist movements.

Mel King is a professor at MIT and director of the Community Fellows program. He has been a local elected official and grass-roots organizer in Boston and led countless electoral and extra-electoral struggles for community reform and advance.

Lydia Sargent edits *Z Magazine* and is a director, playwright, and actor with the Newbury Street Theater in Boston. She has been involved in the feminist and anti-war movements.

Holly Sklar is the author or co-author of several books, including *Washington's War on Nicaragua,* which won an Outstanding Book Award from the Gustavus Myers Center for the Study of Human Rights in the United States. She is a columnist for *Z Magazine.*

Comments By The Authors
On Liberating Theory

Michael Albert: Winning limited respite from harsh oppression is an essential day-to-day priority. But even a brief survey of the recurrence of new forms of old oppressions—new Vietnams, new starvation, new racism, new violence against women, new denials of rights and degradation of potentials—shows that establishing a humane society is the only way to attain lasting liberation. Nonetheless, in recent years "the left" has largely lost its capacity to project an uplifting conception of human possibilities and a plausible picture of how people's potentials might be fulfilled. Since I believe *Liberating Theory* can help reinvigorate our desires for and capacities to achieve a better future, I worked on and advocate its conceptual framework and hope others will do likewise.

Leslie Cagan: Usually my writing focuses on leaflets, organizing materials, calls for action, and fund appeal letters. Working on *Liberating Theory* has allowed us the opportunity to bring together a sample of the diversity of our struggles and has allowed me to think more sharply about theory. The demands of daily political activism and organizing often mean a lack of attention to theory. It is my hope that this collective writing effort will offer social/political activists a nudge in the direction of taking the task of building our theory more seriously.

I believe it will be possible to bring fundamental, revolutionary change to this country. Out of the everyday struggles of people throughout this nation and around the world, we learn new ways to name the problems and define new solutions. At the same time, our organizing and mobilizing needs a framework that gives direction to our efforts.

I hope this book will be read by people active in a wide range of political, social, and economic struggles, as well as those just beginning to think about such issues. This book does not solve the problem or give us magical formulas for organizing. What I hope it does do is provoke discussion, open up debate, motivate further theoretical work and play some role in inspiring us all.

Noam Chomsky: We often tend to focus our attention on today's atrocities and on efforts to mitigate them, at least I do, recognizing, however, that we are at best applying a bandaid to a cancer that will erupt elsewhere. If we are to go beyond, our work must be guided by a vision of a future that is attainable and worth achieving and it must be part of a sustained and long-term commitment by many people, ultimately the great mass of the population, who share this vision.

Liberating Theory is an attempt to come to grips with these problems. I hope that this unusual project will stimulate others to undertake a critical analysis of the ideas presented here and to develop them further and to join in helping to bring this dream a few important steps closer to reality.

Robin Hahnel: Functioning separately, movements to overcome racism, sexism, classism, and authoritarianism fail. Functioning together and sharing aims and methods, they can succeed.

I helped write *Liberating Theory* because I believe that to go forward radically we need to develop a new understanding of society and ourselves suited to human potentials and able to promote solidarity among people with different priorities.

Now that the book exists, I will promote the idea that activists from many constituencies should debate, criticize and improve it in the belief that this can contribute to a growing movement that seeks and finally attains a better future.

Mel King: As an activist, politician, and citizen I constantly enounter people who say injustice exists because people are evil; life can't be better or more fair because that's the way we are. I should be more realistic.

But I know that injustice exists because of the politics of scarcity and its impact on social relations and psychologies—things we can change. I know that life and society can be much better, and that we can make it happen.

Liberating Theory can help us understand society, develop visionary goals, and create effective strategies. Our central aim in writing it was the need to combine agendas of different movements even while preserving the dignity and integrity of each.

My hope for *Liberating Theory* is that it will galvanize anti-racists, feminists, disarmament activists, anti-interventionists, gay and lesbian liberationists, and everyone seeking a better world to live and grow in, helping each with their own priorities and to connect to all the others.

I am a member of the *Rainbow Coalition*. The impetus of the Rainbow is not to reform a little here and a little there, not to, in Vincent Harding's words, have affirmative action in a dehumanized society, but to transform the defining relations of society so that life is vastly improved. *Liberating Theory* provides a way of looking at and thinking about society consistent with my priorities and able to further them. It transcends each of its seven authors to belong to the whole left. I hope readers will respond with support and energy so we can get together and go forward, now.

Lydia Sargent: I could begin with many lofty reasons why I contributed to *Liberating Theory*. But something has happened to them—my lofty reasons, I mean.

As I drift further from the events, ideas, and goals that contributed to my own radical consciousness-raising, I feel more and more impatience, despair, even boredom creeping into my political work and my life and getting a stranglehold on my lofty reasons. I am haunted by the fear that I will live out my life as a witness to the continued existence of what I hate, without ever seeing the fruits of a hoped-for revolution.

So I contributed to *Liberating Theory* for pragmatic as well as lofty reasons. I, frankly, will do anything I can in order *not* to participate in a society that oppresses people around the world while insuring that its own citizens occupy their days with a myriad of limited choices which it refers to as democratic: buying Pepsi or Coke; Evian or Perrier; eating MacDonalds or Burger King; working at Burger King or Wendy's; choosing apartheid or less apartheid; intervention or less intervention; nuclear weapons or more nuclear weapons; straight sex or no sex; profits or more profits; marriage and a career, marriage and no career, no marriage and a career, no marriage and no career; a nice boss or a less nice boss; a job being servile or a servile job; the Vogue version of feminism or the Cosmopolitan version; watching "Kate and Allie" or "Dynasty," *Rambo* or *The Big Chill*; and on and on.

I can no longer rationalize the continued existence of such a society by saying that the opposition is too strong, or the left is too weak, or political disagreements and sectarianism can never be overcome, or we lack a vision, solidarity, courage, commitment, analysis, skills, and knowledge. These are not reasons enough to prevent me believing in the very real possibility of a diverse, creative, liberatory society and in the necessity for all those involved in left political practice to bring their unique perspectives, personalities, and humor to the process of creating and working for such a society. I think the concepts, vision, and strategy discussed in these pages provide a framework not only for beginning but for succeeding.

Holly Sklar: Between the time I finished working on *Liberating Theory* and the writing of this preface, I spent seven weeks in Nicaragua researching a new book on U.S. policy. This was my fourth trip to Nicaragua since 1980, and each time I've come away with an essential message about the power of a people reclaiming their destiny and rebuilding their country from the ground up. Sandinismo is a liberating theory and practice which integrates marxism, feminism, spirituality and cultural liberation, representing a new wisdom etched in Nicaraguan history, but with lessons from and for liberation movements around the world.

We have yet to create our "Sandinismo," our U.S. identity, our liberating program, our popular power. *Liberating Theory* is meant to help close the gaps in our movement and serve as a guide for a movement deserving and capable of taking power and creating a new democracy. *Liberating Theory* rejects dogma and monotony. It was and is a collective venture, a mutual education. We did not take years in an effort to achieve perfect consensus or perfect terminology. Our goal was to achieve a new and valuable synthesis of ideas and concepts, to serve as a catalyst for future endeavors. I think we succeeded in that, and I look forward to new stages of the project, stages molded by additional people and expanding perspectives.

TABLE OF CONTENTS

INTRODUCTION

In the summer of 1984 South End Press asked a number of political activists to plan a collectively-authored book which would analyze conditions in the United States today, project a shared vision of our society as we would like it to be and propose a strategy for bringing about this new society. Over twenty activist/writers from diverse backgrounds agreed to collaborate in this unique effort.

Four participants were chosen by the group to be "core writers," responsible for initiating and revising various drafts of the manuscript. In succeeding months the core writers interviewed the other participants and, had events gone according to plan, the next step would have been to incorporate insights from those interviews into a first draft which would then have been criticized by all participants as if it had been their own work. The core group would next have incorporated suggestions in a new draft and submitted that for further revision. On a few occasions the full collective would have gathered to discuss content and distribution and by the winter of 1985-1986 we would have published the book.

Instead, due to a combination of factors, work stalled shortly after the interviewing ended. The break in the project made us realize that as prospective authors of a political analysis that could unite many constituencies, we first had to agree on a shared conceptual framework for bringing unity out of diversity. But it was clear from our interviews that no one of the many conceptual approaches held by our authors could alone provide guidance. What features define our society? How do they interrelate? These and related questions had to be addressed before we could do more detailed analyses and project goals and strategies. We decided to divide the project into two stages. The first would provide an effective conceptual framework to employ in the second, where we would apply the new insights.

To produce *Liberating Theory*, our shared framework, the original group of "core writers" was enlarged to include all the authors of the present volume: Michael Albert, Leslie Cagan, Noam Chomsky, Robin Hahnel, Mel King, Lydia Sargent, and Holly Sklar. The first draft was written by Albert and Hahnel, and then put through intensive rewrites by the other authors. Not all of us agree with every word and certainly we would each have had different emphases had we written alone. But whatever our differences, we all agree that the framework presented here is a powerful conceptual *starting place* for understanding modern societies, developing liberated visions, and formulating strategies to help us make those visions real. With *Liberating Theory* as a foundation we have high hopes that the product of subsequent efforts will be truly ground-breaking. We fully expect concepts presented here to evolve and new ideas to emerge as the on-going project unfolds.

Chapter One of *Liberating Theory* presents a methodological overview of our perspective. Chapters Two through Five refine and enrich familiar concepts for understanding economic, political, community, and kinship relations. Chapter Six develops new concepts for understanding how these four types of relations influence one another in real societies and chapter Seven addresses questions of historical change. Finally, Chapters Eight and Nine explain how to apply *Liberating Theory*'s conceptual framework to envisioning a liberated society and developing an effective strategy for reaching it: tasks to be undertaken in a second volume.

In a set of appendices, we have also included imaginary dialogues contrasting our perspective to others currently more prevalent on the left. There is one dialogue for each chapter and each dialogue presupposes that the participants have just become familiar with the chapter it relates to. As hypothetical exchanges the dialogues remind us that ideas are held by people and that concepts for movements must be thrashed out in context of real needs. But including the dialogues was the most contested decision we had to make. While four of us thought of the dialogues as provocative concluding sections for each chapter— Albert, Chomsky, Hahnel, and Sargent—the other three—Cagan, King, and Sklar—found them to be, at best, distracting and, at worst, caricatures. Favoring "participatory democracy," we decided to include them as appendices at the end of the whole volume to allow readers to make their own decisions about whether and/or when to read them.

Liberating Theory emphasizes methods, not final answers. It does not analyze specific events, but presents *ways of understanding* past and present events as well as possible futures. It does not develop a particular strategy, but presents methods for creating diverse strategies suited to complex contexts.

In light of our ultimate desire to apply this book's concepts to fresh analysis and organizing, we are circulating the manuscript to our original list of authors (as well as others) and asking each to decide whether they want to re-commit themselves to the second stage of this project, the work that will develop more detailed strategy and vision, using *Liberating Theory* as a guide. We hope the next book will be available by Fall 1987.

Readers can help us pursue this ambitious goal by writing to the Collective Book Project, c/o South End Press. We welcome criticisms of *Liberating Theory* as well as ideas for the forthcoming work. Naturally, we hope these books will make a powerful contribution to left vision, strategy, and solidarity.

CHAPTER ONE

METHOD, MOTIVATION AND SOCIAL THEORY

Political activists need concepts suited to accurately analyzing society and history. But accuracy is not all that matters. In addition, to help popular movements, clear and concise concepts need to be applicable by activists operating in everyday situations—not just by "armchair" radicals with endless time for deciphering arcane rhetoric. Moreover, social theory must help prevent the "baggage of history" from subverting attempts to establish liberating new relations. To be liberatory, concepts need to counter tendencies to ignore, devalue, or oversimplify important social dynamics such as race, sex, class, or authority. This point cannot be emphasized enough: activist theory must help its advocates overcome their own oppressive socializations. It will not do for our theories to aggravate or even impose new biases.

Certainly social theories cannot help us make *testable* predictions in the manner of physics or chemistry. Social predictions cannot approach the precision of a formula: "if we mix chemicals A and B in environment X, after a said time elapses, such and such amount of C will result." But, nonetheless, we can use powerful social theory to explain relationships; to envision possibilities and delineate trends that may impede or promote those possibilities; and to make "probabilistic predictions" about likely outcomes of current activities—all in ways that broaden our perspectives and counter our biases. These are our goals for "liberating theory."

5

Our Search For New Concepts

When marxists conceptualize society, a particular picture of social and historical possibilities emerges. Is the marxist view comprehensive enough to meet activists' needs? Does it counter or aggravate socialized biases? What about other theories such as feminism, nationalism, anarchism, populism or ecologism? Advocates of different schools of thought rarely claim to already have all the answers we need about history, contemporary societies, or alternative visions. They often do claim, however, to have conceptual frameworks sufficient for developing these answers now and in the future. Our view is different. While these theories teach many important truths, they also bias our analyses by obscuring some important dynamics and unduly exaggerating others. We feel that not only do we need new answers about our society but also new concepts to help us find those answers. Let's look at this problem more closely.

Neither Monist Nor Pluralist Methods

At the extreme, some political activists claim that *one* particular domination precipitates all really important oppressions. Whether marxist, anarchist, nationalist or feminist, these "ideal types" argue that important social relations can all be *reduced* to the economy, state, culture *or* gender. Their extreme "monist" approaches emphasize "reductionist" foundations.

Each idealized monist theory targets different "domination relations" as the "motor force of history." Not surprisingly, as they each find a different essential tension, their respective proponents criticize one another harshly. The idealized marxist looks first to economic and class relations to explain not only economic, but also sexual, racial, political and all other types of domination. Likewise, the idealized feminist looks primarily to gender, the idealized nationalist to culture, and the idealized anarchist to the state. Of course, only a few activists actually assert that everything, everywhere is always economy-based, state-based, gender-based, *or* culture-based—and nothing more. These ideal types are caricatures. But most adherents of each perspective do claim that their particular concepts of structure and power are at least *the* central determinants of oppression and social change.

For example, some people adopt a label like "feminist" simply to show their commitment to overcoming a particular form of oppression without necessarily accepting only one theoretical paradigm as valid. They may mean to convey, for example, that they see the roots of

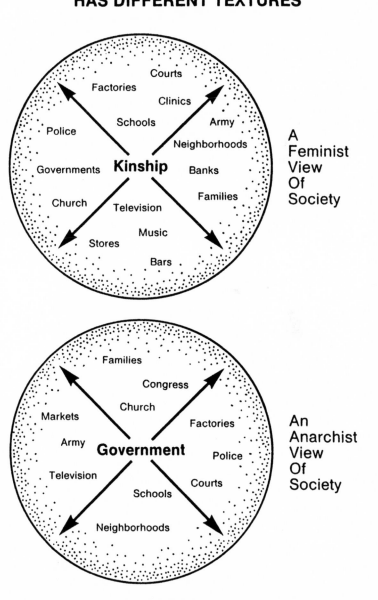

VIEWED FROM DIFFERENT CONCEPTUAL PERSPECTIVES, SOCIETY HAS DIFFERENT TEXTURES

A Feminist View Of Society

Kinship — Courts, Factories, Clinics, Schools, Police, Army, Neighborhoods, Governments, Banks, Church, Families, Television, Music, Stores, Bars

An Anarchist View Of Society

Government — Families, Congress, Church, Markets, Factories, Army, Police, Television, Courts, Schools, Neighborhoods patriarchy as having powerful influences on all sides of social life, while still acknowledging that other critical dynamics might also be at work. But many other activists adopt "ism" labels to make the self-conscious theoretical claim that a particular sphere of society deserves priority attention because it incorporates the driving forces which determine historical possibilities in every sphere of society. A feminist of this sort might "seek the ultimate cause and the great moving power of all historic events in the dialectic of sex; the division of society into two distinct biological classes for procreative reproduction, and the struggles of those classes with one another; in the changes in the modes of marriage, reproduction and childcare...; in the connected development of other physically-differentiated classes (castes); and in the first division of labor based on sex which developed into the (economic-cultural) class system."[1]

The monist/reductionist program always has roughly the same structure: a body of experience or data is dissected into components, some of which are said to have features that disproportionately determine the properties of the whole they together compose. The whole is then analyzed primarily in terms of these favored parts, on the grounds that these parts exist in and of themselves, operate largely according to their own laws, and powerfully influence the whole by processes immune to major alteration by operations of other parts of the whole. Though monist analysts distinguish themselves by choosing *different* defining features of society and history, their basic method is the same.

No matter how carefully they proceed, all the different reductions of the same complex phenomena to different root causes cannot be correct. Naturally, representatives of different perspectives ably criticize economics and only influenced secondarily by gender, culture and polity, and also primarily by gender, but only secondarily by economics, polity, and culture. Not all reductions can be simultaneously correct. Representatives of different perspectives naturally ably criticize one another. In the ensuing chaos many disgruntled leftists opt for eclectic pluralism, employing the concepts of more than one framework, much as the anarchist Bakunin called himself a marxist in economics, and as many marxist economists now call themselves feminists regarding gender.

Countering monism, pluralist approaches claim we must use more than one set of intellectual tools because social causes cannot be reduced to a single class of determining relations. Many activists simultaneously claim to be marxist and feminist, anarchist and nationalist, or

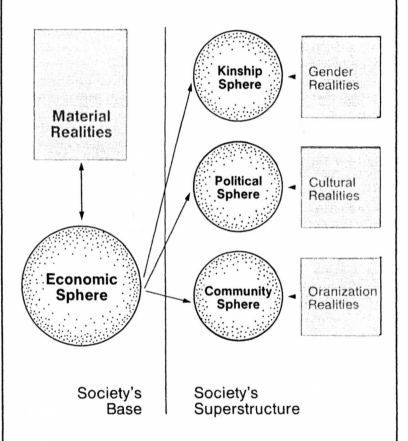

SUBTLE MONIST CONCEPTUALIZATION ECONOMIC VERSION

Material Realities

Kinship Sphere — Gender Realities

Political Sphere — Cultural Realities

Economic Sphere

Community Sphere — Oranization Realities

Society's Base | Society's Superstructure

To portray other "versions" leave
Main Elements in place and simply exchange
"Economic Sphere" and "Material Realities" labels
for any of their Kinship, Politics, or Community
counterparts

feminist and anarchist, because they rightly recognize the complexity of their environment and see merit in more than one analytic orientation. Whether a pluralist analysis succeeds obviously depends upon the analyst's skill in choosing the right tools to scrutinize changing circumstances. Yet pluralism dictates that to analyze the economy you should use marxist categories while to analyze the family you should use feminist categories, and this advice is inadequate.

Monist approaches fail whenever we need to recognize more than one set of causal factors. For example, black and white and male and female workers don't all have the same interests and mindsets simply because they all belong to the same economic class. Over-simplifying causal factors to include only class relations ignores racial and sexual dynamics that cause women and blacks, among others, to endure different oppressions, not only when pay checks and pink slips are dispersed, but day-in and day-out because of the racist and sexist definitions of their economic tasks. Class concepts cannot alone adequately explain factory life and so, *even to understand the economy*, much less the rest of society, we must go beyond marxism. Similarly, each monist approach exaggerates the influence of its favored sphere, underestimates the influence of other spheres, and largely ignores the crucial fact that every sphere is itself critically influenced by other sources of social definition.

Pluralist approaches try to escape these distortions by adopting more than one perspective, but since events are often so multifaceted that only a comprehensive theory can reveal their true character, this too often fails. Imagine looking at a country scene using, in turn, blue, red and green filters. Though you would see much, you would also have great difficulty discerning features dependent upon how colors *mix*. Similarly, a marxist-feminist will see traditional economic exploitation and also patriarchal violence against women, but miss many of the more subtle ways that gender relations redefine class definitions or that economic dynamics redefine family norms.

Because they fail to account for multi-faceted defining influences, marxist categories insufficiently explain even the economy, feminist categories insufficiently explain even gender, nationalist categories insufficiently explain even culture, and anarchist categories insufficiently explain even the state. All these foci are certainly necessary, but to use them optimally we need to develop a new orientation that allows us to embody refined versions of each primary framework in *a new whole*.

A PLURALIST CONCEPTUALIZATION

Material Realities

Cultural Realities

Organization Realities

Gender Realities

Economic Sphere

Community Sphere

Political Sphere

Kinship Sphere

Social Life And Change

Complementary Holism

We tentatively call this new orientation complementary holism. It is rooted in two modern scientific principles: "holism" and "complementarity." *Holism* informs us that reality's many parts always act together to form an entwined whole. In the words of physicist David Bohm, all phenomena are "to be understood not as...independently and permanently existent but rather as product[s] that [have been] formed in the whole flowing movement and that will ultimately dissolve back into that movement."[2] Of course Bohm doesn't mean to imply that a useful understanding of an electron in a lab of a physicist in N.Y. can't be had unless we also explain the texture of wood in a staircase in the Kremlin. The influences of the latter will be too slight to care about. But he does mean to highlight that, since all phenomena influence all other phenomena, we should always be very careful about how we abstract any particular aspect of our surroundings from the whole. Extracting the economy from the rest of society, for example, will often be ill advised. Here the interactions are too important to exclude any from our focus. Since in practice it is not so easy to keep this rather obvious guideline in mind, choosing concepts that continually highlight its importance can help.

Complementarity, in the sense we use it, means that the parts which compose wholes interrelate to help define one another, even though each appears often to have an independent and even contrary existence. Our definition, as further developed below, is a somewhat altered form of the general complementarity principle developed by scientist Niels Bohr and other members of what is called the "Copenhagen School," who felt the more precise quantum physics definition of complementarity was generalizable to various social and historical phenomena.

Just as Marx and Engels paid strict attention to "state of the art" science in their time, we should keep up with contemporary developments. Ironically, however, though most contemporary marxists pride themselves on being "scientific," few bother to notice that "state of the art" science has changed dramatically in the last hundred years. While avoiding simplistic mimicry and misapplication of scientific principles, we should update our methods by seriously examining contemporary science for new ideas relevant to our theoretical efforts.

Modern quantum physics, for example, teaches that reality is not a collection of separate entities but a vast and intricate "unbroken whole." Ilya Prigogine comments, "The new paradigms of science may be expected to develop into the new science of connectedness which means the recognition of unity in diversity."[3] When thinking about phenomena, we inevitably conceptually abstract parts from the whole in which they reside, but they then exist as separate entities only in our perceptions. There are no isolated electrons, for example, only fields of force continually ebbing and flowing in a seamless web of activity which manifests events that we choose to call electrons because it suits our analytic purposes. For the physicist, each electron, quark, or whatever is a "process" and a "network." As a process it has a developmental trajectory—extending through all time. As a network, it is part of an interactive pattern—stretching throughout all space. Every part embodies and is subsumed in a larger whole.

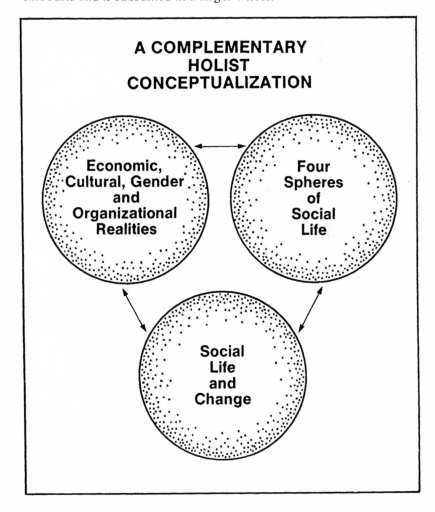

Similarly, relativity theorists explain that our image of time as a continually progressing river is also a human construct. In reality, time no more flows than does space. The two are complementary aspects of a single whole, even as we perceive them to be separate. In both spatial and temporal dimensions there exists only unity in diversity, diversity in unity.

Using similar logic, contrary to most radical formulations, we argue that it is wrong to call a society "capitalist," or "patriarchal," or "racist" or "dictatorial," and think that with a single descriptor one has revealed the essence of the society in question. Many readers might be thinking, "that's obvious; who could disagree?" Yet, a review of radical literature shows that the answer is, at least in practice, a great many people. In publication after publication, a single sphere of society is addressed (or even labeled) and claims are then made to the effect that not only has this particular sphere of society been fully understood—which it hasn't—but that the fundamental dynamics of the overall society have been properly illuminated. Writing a book on economics or culture is fine. We cannot always address everything. Examining single spheres in isolation with monist theories and claiming comprehensive knowledge is not fine. We needn't abstract poorly.

Adrienne Rich's eloquent definition of patriarchy provides an example of monistic over-generalization:

> Patriarchy is the power of the fathers: a familial-social, ideological, political system in which men—by force, direct pressure, or through ritual, tradition, law, and language, customs, etiquette, education, and the division of labor, determine what part women shall or shall not play, and in which the female is everywhere subsumed under the male... Under patriarchy, I may live in *purdah* or drive a truck;...I may serve my husband his early-morning coffee within the clay walls of a Berber village or march in an academic procession; whatever my status or situation, my derived economic class, or my sexual preference, I live under the power of the fathers, and I have access only to so much of privilege or influence as the patriarchy is willing to accede to me, and only for so long as I will pay the price for male approval.[4]

From this starting point, if we are not very careful, it is all too easy to lose track of the defining influence economic, political, and cultural forms can have on gender relations and lose track of the different experiences of different women, of the different possibilities they face, and so on. Yet, often we do need to temporarily escape the complexities of "connectedness," and at these times we take as our focus not the whole interconnected society, but a particular type of abstract economy, kinship system, cultural process or governing form. We write a treatise on the "capitalist economy" or "parliamentary democracy" just as a physicist might write one on the "electron." Yet, in doing so we must remember that our conclusions are suspect. For as with the electron and its field, the economy, community, state and kinship spheres are always complementary facets of a single unbroken natural and social order.

Of course, we are not saying that a theory of the electron is suspect if it doesn't include reflections on the Crusades—just that it is suspect if it doesn't include reflections on photons or even gravitation. And likewise, we are not saying a theory of the capitalist firm is suspect if it does not include reflections on the anthropology of ancient matriarchal societies. But it had better include reflections on contemporary gender, community and political relations since these always intertwine with and help define economic forms.

To take the economic example further, the assumption that only classes are important economic actors and that classes are wholly defined by economic relationships common to different modes of production would be valid only if it were justifiable to abstract from the fact that members of classes are also members of different sexes, cultural communities, and political structures. That is, racial, gender, political and other dynamics which play upon economic relations would have to be marginal for the theory to always do a good job. Yet, all too often such abstractions are flawed, as when many marxists assume the lack of relevance of gender in assessing production relations or when many feminists ignore race when assessing kinship forms.

In short, since society itself is holistic, it is essential that we develop an intellectual framework *specifically contoured to understanding an interconnected reality.* We should expect interdependence and only introduce simplifying assumptions that deny the importance of interconnections when such assumptions are carefully justified. Since existing theories fail to adequately follow this approach, we cannot begin our efforts by assuming marxism, feminism, nationalism, anarchism or even some combination of these.

Contemporary science teaches us to examine reality in unusual ways. Embarking upon our effort to create a new conceptual framework for political analysis, we should heed its lessons. Unlike monists, we must incorporate more than one angle of approach. Unlike pluralists, we must integrate our diverse angles of approach and allow each to refine the others within a comprehensive framework which allows important truths to emerge.

Dissipative Systems

Thermodynamics, which is concerned primarily with energy relations, is another physical science with methodological insights of use to social theorists. Here, Ilya Prigogine's studies have led to a new theory of change of what he calls "dissipative systems."

For Prigogine, most dissipative systems continually undergo reproductive transformations. Continual fluxes in dissipative systems embody a perpetual flow of energy and matter which leave the dissipative systems largely unchanged over time. Though everything flows, the result of this turmoil is only *evolutionary change* fluctuating around a stable pattern of development which defines the character of the whole dynamic system. People, for example, undergo countless flows of energy, material and information with the surrounding environment, yet each morning we awake with our identity secure. Viewed one way we are wildly out of equilibrium, our very cells regularly dying off and being replaced. Yet, viewed another way, we are here today, tomorrow and the day after, relatively unchanged.

Sometimes, however, fluctuations in dissipative systems invoke fundamental transformations in their defining characteristics. In these "revolutionary" cases, instead of all changes away from the basic defining pattern being reigned in, pressures from within and without together push the system so far from its defining trajectory that old identities shatter.

Prigogine applies his conceptualization universally, to the smallest physical systems, to individuals and social groups, to societies and whole ecologies, and to cosmic systems. In biological and social *evolution*, for example, changes occur within limits and generally preserve the host system's defining character. In biological and social *revolution*, however, changes burst all restraints so the host system ceases to exist in its old form and is replaced instead by a new system with new defining features and altered evolutionary and revolutionary potentials. Though it would be simple-minded to extrapolate too freely from Prigogine's studies, his lessons can provide insights relevant to our own understanding of social systems.

If we view all complex structures as dissipative systems, following Prigogine, then we can evolve an image of social structures existing within, overlapping and encompassing one another, all influencing and even flowing through one another. On occasion, the ebb and flow of one sphere becomes so pronounced—owing to its own internal motions and/or to growing pressures from without—that it undergoes a profound change and, in turn, sometimes causes other systems to change as well. Seeing societies and even parts of societies—like their kinship spheres or economies—as dissipative systems should prove enlightening in coming chapters. Moreover, although the specific features of revolutionary processes differ depending on the type of "dissipative system" under discussion, the general dynamic is always present.

Yet, if nature is an unbroken whole with parts we can only examine in light of how they mutually interpenetrate and define one another, what does it mean to discuss a "system" separate from the rest of nature? We don't hesitate to speak of chemical compounds, molecules, biological organs, rocks, mountains, products, people, economies and societies as separate "things." In each case, however, we mentally extricate a conceptual piece from the whole tapestry of society and nature where no such extrication is entirely accurate. We do this, of course, because our mental abstraction helps us think about the part, albeit a little incorrectly, in a more manageable way. If every time we wanted to talk about a chair, car, or friend we had to simultaneously discuss the whole rest of our society and even of the universe, obviously we would never say or think anything.

At the other end of this axis, however, as we have already argued, it is also wrong to forget that a tapestry of interconnections does exist, so that whenever we do speak of parts by themselves, we do so only in approximate ways. We must always check to see that the interconnections we ignore can, indeed, be ignored at small cost. To initiate our theoretical journeys with reductionist assumptions that unchanging "atoms" of influence will be found at the foundation of all social and historical processes would be a disastrously narrowing step. A more encompassing attitude informed by a desire to carefully search out justifiable abstractions is better suited to activist needs.

When we extract a part from a larger whole and examine it, we must remain aware that an encompassing whole defines the aspect we analyze. Indeed, for Prigogine, precisely the relationship of the part to the whole—the way its aspects interrelate and flow through that whole and vice versa—allows the part to attain sufficient coherence for us to examine it separately. If we think of ourselves again, it is the way energy and materials flow from our environment through us and back allowing us to continually reproduce our component features that allow us to maintain our coherent definition as separate people. Likewise, thinking of an economy, it is the particular ways goods, services, ideas, and relations flow though the economy, from it to the rest of society and back, that allows the sphere to maintain its coherence. Without interconnection and continual flux, neither people nor economies could persist as discernible systems with defining patterns of development to be maintained during normal times and transformed during revolutionary times. In essence, it is a special type of ongoing change that promotes ongoing continuity.

Within dissipative systems, parts are always subsumed under still larger wholes and any boundaries we recognize must be understood as abstractions. It follows that when we try to understand any particular system's evolutionary and revolutionary tendencies we should look not only to its "internal" attributes, but also to those affecting it from "without." Indeed, the division between "within" and "without" is really only something that we impose by our particular conceptual labeling of the system. This lesson is important when talking about such societal subsystems as the economy, polity, community and kinship spheres and can go a long way toward preventing monist misconceptualizations. For example, this recognition runs counter to the idea of employing exclusively an "internal contradictions" view as the basis of a methodology of change, precisely because the concept "internal" is itself an arbitrary one dependent upon how we view society, history, or whatever subject matter we are addressing. For by our conceptualizing, it is we who define the boundaries between "things" determining what is "internal" and "external" to each. Again, we can and certainly should do this for many purposes, but not always, and always with great care.

Fundamentals of Complementary Holism

Many different kinds of domination characterize human history. Imperialist powers have dominated other peoples politically, culturally, and economically. Within particular nations, men have dominated women, ruling classes have dominated other classes, whites have dominated people of color, members of one religion have dominated members of another, and so on. Moreover, each of these different kinds of domination has existed in a variety of forms; each has had pervasive effects on the quality of people's lives; and each has influenced the whole structure of societies in which they have appeared. Genocide, colonialism, slavery, racism, and religious oppression have each had their own particular dynamics and consequences. Rape, psychological abuse, objectification, and the exclusion of women from participation in political, cultural, or economic activity outside the family, as well as discrimination against women when they are able to participate in "public" life, present a multitude of different forms of gender oppression. The exploitation of peasants by landlords, workers by capitalists and workers by planning bureaucracies and managers are all forms of class oppression, each different from the others. Similarly, execution, imprisonment, banning of political activity, and unjust access to public participation are all forms of state opression, any of which can be utilized by monarchies, dictatorships, representative "democracies," or even participatory democracies. Our pains have come in many shapes and sizes, each with their own characteristic signatures and each with influences extending far beyond their immediate spheres.

Each of these types of domination has elicited a monist theory— feminism, nationalism, anarchism, marxism—which we have rejected as inadequate whether taken separately or in pluralist combination. In coming chapters, we outline alternative concepts that start from the premise that *each domination generates highly interconnected but irreducible social forces.* We also build a series of sub-theories that make no *a priori* assumptions about any hierarchy of different forms of domination, a view we will support in more detail later. Only empirical investigation of a particular society at a particular time can verify the existence or non-existence of a hierarchy of dominations in that particular case. And often, rather than a hierarchy of oppressions, there will be a holistic interweaving of oppressions.

Center and Boundary

As a complex "dissipative system," any society usually evolves along a relatively stable pattern of steady evolutionary change. People engage in diverse types of social activity which leads to the creation of systems and institutions which generate social groups with different social responsibilities and different access to status, power, and means of attaining well being. Occasionally, these component structures and even society as a whole undergo revolutionary transformations.

Using vague "domination terminology," we can say that any society has a well-defined complex of social relationships determining its "modes of domination" and division of its citizenry into groups of dominators and dominated. When a society merely evolves, these patterns reproduce without major change. But when a revolution occurs, they transform.

We can conceive of society as two basic networks: a human *center* composed of citizens, their consciousnesses, personalities, needs and skills, and a surrounding institutional *boundary* composed of society's institutions and their role structures. These two networks, the human and the institutional, "us" and "the system," together comprise the larger society which, in turn, encompasses both. The institutions are certainly created by the actions and expectations of the human population. Yet, the consciousnesses and personalities of the people are themselves molded by the institutional structures people continually confront.

The psychological dynamics that equilibrate our personalities and society's boundary vary, to be sure, but the basic relations are simple. By our activities we not only fulfill immediate needs, but also develop personality traits and future preferences. When we work in a certain type of job, or mother or father children, or go to church, temple or mosque, or participate in politics, we not only influence others but also "create" ourselves "to fit." When we contour our activities to fulfill certain role requirements, we naturally acquire certain related traits and needs. Moreover, as we have a disposition to think well of ourselves, most often we then also contour our attitudes to rationalize our efforts so they appear logical, good, or at least necessary.

It follows that if institutions offer only a limited number of roles through which we may gain access to means of survival and fulfillment, most of us will naturally and inexorably mold ourselves to fit the requirements of those roles. If we do otherwise, we either become permanent misfits or we seek to change our institutional context. So, most often, most people develop acceptable self-images by accommodating their values to the logic of their activities, which are in turn structured by society's institutional boundary. And this means that we regularly bring our mindsets into accord with that boundary. Most times, therefore, powerful pressures push people to seek only what society is prepared to bestow upon them.

At the same time, institutions obviously also reflect the personalities and ideas we bring to their design and construction. We continually recreate our society's institutions so that of course they accord with our values, needs and desires.

In sum, both society's boundary and its center create and are created by the other; each is the subject and object of their entwined history. The two *co-define* one another. The division between them is imposed and porous. If we extend center and boundary in time and space, they each expand through their "edges" to embody one another.

Society's center and boundary are *complementary* aspects of a single unbroken whole. Both center and boundary are complex dissipative systems. Whatever society's defining features may be, they will necessarily pervade both society's center and boundary. They will persist through evolutionary changes since such changes necessarily involve limited adaptations of both center and boundary. Revolution, however, will alter these defining features. Since we know that historically people universally engage in certain social activities, which in turn involve social relations contouring daily life and governing group interactions, as our next conceptual step it makes sense to sub-divide society along lines highlighting these activities, social relations, and social groups. In the next four chapters we will conceptualize economic, political, kinship and community spheres showing how each may be usefully characterized by a predominant activity and particular defining social relations and group structures—*each entwined with the others in a complementary holist fashion.* We will not assume at the outset any particular hierarchy of the influences stemming from these spheres, but will instead address such interrelations as we come upon them in our theorizing. After discussing each sphere largely in isolation from the others in these early chapters, later we will attain a higher level of accuracy by combining our new conceptualizations into an encompassing framework for thinking about societies and history.

*Please Note: Readers who would now like to consider a hypothetical dialogue dealing with issues raised in chapter one should turn to page 148. Others may prefer to read all the dialogues at once, after having completed the main body of text.

CHAPTER TWO
COMMUNITY

In our framework, "communities" are groups of people who share a common sense of historical identity or heritage. Usually this shared identity derives from a common culture, language or lifestyle developed while the original members of the community lived in geographical proximity. A nation, for example, is a particular type of community comprised of an organized society of people, with a common territory and government. In turn, within nations, we find additional distinct types of communities and sub-communities based on ethnicity, cultural heritage, race, locale, etc., and these may conform with or cut across class and sex lines. We claim that identification with one or more communities has important social implications for people's needs, desires, responsibilities, manners of ritual and celebration, and ways of accommodating to diverse institutional requirements.

Certainly the universality of many communities makes their existence *appear* more biological than historical. And, indeed, it is also true that when, where and by whom we are born does tend to predispose us to become members of particular communities. Nonetheless, closer attention to the phenomenon of becoming a community member reveals that we develop our community identifications, not biologically, but by adopting particular cultural beliefs and behaviors and that communities evolve through a combination of internal and external *social* relations. Social relations, not genes, define community allegiances.

23

The Concept Of A "Community Sphere"

We know that national communities develop their sense of a shared history owing to geographical constancy and common language and culture, as in France, for example. In contrast, we also know that religious communities can be defined by common spiritual beliefs and customs as for practitioners of Zen Buddhism, or by the religion of their mother, as for Jews. Ethnic communities in turn identify through shared origin in some geographically defined community, like Poland, while specifically racial communities, we will argue, are defined more by the character of their relations with other communities than by internal characteristics, as Blacks in the U.S. or Chinese in Vietnam.

Within the borders of the United States, we know that there are numerous Indian nations, struggling to see their sovereign rights to land and self-determination realized. We also know that Blacks, Latino/as and Asian Americans form racial communities, themselves made up of distinct sub-communities rooted in nationality: Afro-Americans, Haitians, Chicanos, Puerto Ricans, Chinese, Japanese, Filipinos. In turn, Italian, Irish and Polish Americans are among the many different white ethnic communities while Protestants, Catholics, Muslims and Jews make up different religious communities, and New Englanders, Southerners, Mid-Westerners and Westerners form different regional communities. South Boston, East Boston and Boston's "North End" represent different neighborhood communities. Other kinds of cultural communities are WASP, Yuppy, Punk, Hip-Hop, etc. And finally, we also know that these far from homogeneous communities exert widely divergent, changing influences on people and society.

It follows from all this common knowledge that we need a concept of the community sphere because in human societies people—whatever their economic, gender or political affiliations—also develop important beliefs, needs, desires and behavior patterns corresponding to particular community roles. Moreover, people bring these community traits to all their life activities. What we mean by the "community sphere" is thus the network of all these communities and their intra- and interrelations.

The Importance Of The Community Sphere

Clearly, any society will vary greatly depending on whether its members share a single religious afffiliation, ethnic identification, or racial heritage or, instead, belong to many religious, ethnic, and racial communities. Similarly, life in a particular society will vary dramatically depending on the nature of its community relations with other societies. Moreover, these types of variations can be as critical to social possibilities as others deriving from class, gender or governance. It follows that to characterize a society's state, economic or kinship institutions, or even all three, without characterizing its community institutions, will not yield a comprehensive picture.

Moreover, there are important differences between the cultures of different religions, ethnic groups, regions, and nations. Different communities have different interpretations of history, philosophies of life and death, and values relating to material wealth, personal relationships, scientific knowledge, nature, and family. Communities with different cultural attitudes toward property, will likely develop different economic spheres even if they share many defining forms. Contrast the economic role of land in Indian and capitalist non-Indian economies. Communities that place different cultural values on family relations will likely develop different kinship spheres, even though they may share basic patriarchal gender structures. Consider variations in family roles between whites and blacks in the U.S.

But community differences arise both from differences in internally elaborated characteristics and from the interface between communities. All too often, for example, one community may fear a threatened invasion by another, or two communities may have different beliefs and customs, and each may worry that the other will impose its values and entice away community members. But whatever the real or imagined causes, hostility across community boundaries can have profound effects, including wars, followed by the assimilation or annihilation of one community by another. Or, short of such intense conflict, the internal evolution of community/cultural forms can nonetheless be disfigured by the cultural products of an outward facing hostility. For example, how communities view each other can affect how each views itself. We need only think of the history of some of the world's most troubled communities—such as Israeli Jews and Palestinian Arabs, or Northern Irish Catholics and Northern Irish Protestants—for examples of this powerful dynamic.

In coming chapters we will argue that the consciousness and needs of members of different genders and classes can be conditioned by their struggles with one another over values, roles, and wealth. In this chapter we see that the same can be true of communities. They too may form in opposition to one another and develop self-identities in part determined by the character of the struggles between them. So it is that we need to pay special attention to "community" and the "community sphere" in our efforts to understand society and history. For this sphere is critically important in determining how we live and how our societies change over time.

The Origins Of Community Identifications

People form communities because community activity is central to the process of human social definition. Humans must learn what social roles to play since, unlike bees, for example, our genes do not make some of us "queens" and others "drones" or "workers." Bees and humans both satisfy needs through elaborate social activity, yet the manner in which bees and people create their sociality differs profoundly. Groups of bees have no need to generate a sense of their particular historical identity to carry out their activities as a hive. Groups of people, however, do need to generate a sense of their historical continuity and identity through cultural activity.

Although inter-community relations can make people insular, hostile to one another and racist, and although intra-community relations can organize cultural activity, such as religion, in a sexist, close-minded, or otherwise hierarchical way, the ongoing activity of forming communities also often meets many positive human needs. Indeed, historically we form communities precisely as a means to attain cultural and emotional continuity in a conscious, profoundly human, emphatically social way. Community is certainly not instrinsically bad. And to fully understand any facet of the critical causes and consequences of cultural activity, we must surely work to understand the positive as well as the negative. For often, even the most negative inter- and intra-community relations are linked to people's struggles to cope with fundamental questions of life and death, and search for social solidarity.

Race and Racism

Most people think of race as a biological differentiation. You are what you are by virtue of birth. Yet, the purely genetic differences between members of different groups of people traditionally labeled "races"—as measured by averages over the groups—proves to be less by chemical composition and type, by a large margin, than the genetic differences among diverse members of a particular race. That is, the differences between two randomly selected white people are likely to be greater than the differences between the average genetic characteristics—if they are discernable at all—for blacks and whites, Native Americans and Asians, and so on.

The division of the human species into races is biologically— *though not socially*—arbitrary. We could differentiate humans along countless axes, such as height, weight and other physical features. If we assigned racial categories to groups of humans with different heights— for example, for every foot of height from four feet up determines a new race—we would be more biologically precise than the usual racial designation by skin color. For no fixed biological boundary exists between Asian and Caucasian, black and Indian, whereas a fixed boundary does exist between those who are shorter than five feet and those who are between five and six feet. Races are simply cultural communities which have historically come to be identified by physical ascriptions. Racism is the ordering of these communities in a hierarchy in which those "above" deem those "below" genetically inferior.

Community Oppressions And Resistance

The fact that relations between communities always influence both and that communities ultimately exist for natural and positive reasons should not lead us to a false conclusion of symmetry or to a false optimism that community dynamics will always be positive. Communities can adopt oppressive norms internally and, moreover, whenever one community dominates another not only will the symmetry between their social positions break down, so will the symmetry of internal effects.

Regarding colonialism, for example, one of the most oppressive community relationships, Frantz Fanon writes in *The Wretched of the Earth*:

> Because it is a systematic negation of the other person and a
> furious determination to deny the other person all attributes
> of humanity, colonialism forces the people it dominates to
> ask themselves the question constantly: "In reality, who am
> I?"[1]

In Fanon's Algeria, as with every colonial situation, the struggle for liberation is a struggle against internalized oppression as well as against the colonial oppressor. From the perspective of the subjugated community, the choice is either submission, with all its physical and psychological pain, or resistance.

Paulo Freire writes, in *Pedagogy of the Oppressed*:

> The oppressed suffer from the duality which has established itself in their innermost being. They discover that without freedom they cannot exist authentically. Yet, although they desire authentic existence, they fear it. They are at one and the same time themselves and the oppressor whose consciousness they have internalized. The conflict lies in the choice between being wholly themselves or being divided; between ejecting the oppressor within or not ejecting him; between human solidarity or alienation; between following prescriptions or having choices; between being spectators or actors; between acting or having the illusion of acting through the action of the oppressors; between speaking out or being silent, castrated in their power to create and re-create, in their power to transform the world.[2]

In the relationship between oppressor and oppressed, it is the oppressed who must overcome the dehumanization of both. The oppressors must continue to oppress the subjugated community if they are to maintain their economic, political and cultural power and privilege. The oppressors cannot renounce their power and privilege *within* a racist relationship; they must *abandon* that relationship. And while there are inspiring cases of individuals abandoning their racist heritage—South African whites, for example, who work with the liberation struggle—there is no historical example of genuine, peaceful abdication of racist supremacy by the whole ruling group. Freire writes:

> Dehumanization, which marks not only those whose humanity has been stolen, but also (though in a different way) those who have stolen it, is a *distortion* of the vocation of becoming more fully human... This, then, is the great humanistic and historical task of the oppressed: to liberate themselves and their oppressors as well.[3]

Community activity defines a sphere of social life that causes the formation of groups who share common aims and desires, who sometimes oppress others, rebel, and/or attain liberation. It must be a focus of radical attention. But with what priority and methodology?

Nationalism As A Kind of Monism

Nationalists focus on the community sphere as the site of critical causal influence in history and *rightfully* argue that cultural identifications cause people to have different values and ways of thinking that help delimit how we live. Nationalists also *rightfully* argue that cultural attitudes permeate not just community, but all social spheres—economic, political, and kinship. It is nationalists, for example, who most emphatically show how racism and apartheid differentially redefine many capitalist and patriarchal norms in both South Africa and the U.S.

However, having developed these powerful insights, the temptation arises for nationalists to over-extend their recognitions to arrive at the erroneous conclusion that community relations *alone* define social life. "Community is base, the rest superstructure." "Sexism is a cultural disease confined to white communities." "Class differentiations arise out of community exploitation." There is a temptation to leap from seeing *a* centrally defining relation—which evidence supports—to identifying *the* primary relation exercising an asymmetrical influence on all other social relations—which evidence denies. And, understandably, nationalists are even more tempted to take this leap when they so often encounter Eurocentric social theories which haughtily refuse to grant cultures status even as one centrally defining relation among many.

Still, this ideal "culturalism" is myopic. It over-exaggerates community activity, and, in turn, underestimates the effect of other spheres on community relations themselves. Practitioners tend not to fully realize the importance of phenomena associated with sexism and class oppressions and to overlook the many class, gender, and political schisms that can divide members of communities against one another. To get beyond these weaknesses without denying the integrity of cultural forces and losing the insights nationalism offers is the goal liberated concepts must attain. It is necessary, therefore, for us to elaborate community concepts which are able to recognize that communities always embody economic, gender, and state functions and to reflect the influence of forces arising from these spheres on communities as well as vice versa.

Conclusion

Every human society generates a sense of its particular historical heritage through cultural activity. This highly social interaction in turn creates distinct communities whose inter-relations have included some of the most powerful dominance relations in human history. Community relations critically affect our lives, but it is wrong to think different racial, religious, or national communities are homogeneous in the sense that each member faces essentially identical life prospects simply by virtue of being Black, Protestant or Irish. Communities fracture internally along gender and class lines, just as genders and classes fracture internally along community lines. What's more, communities also internally fracture along community lines. For example, though the label "Catholic" defines a community for some purposes, it is not only true that people experience Catholicism differently if they are male or female, but also if they are Black or white. Ultimately, we must carefully examine the internal characteristics of each community and also the nature of the interfaces between communities and with gender, economic, and political spheres to successfully develop a thorough understanding of any society.

The community sphere is certainly institutionally diffuse containing a variety of religious, ethnic, and geographical elements. Nevertheless, community activity is essential to life and irreducible to any other kind of activity. Community dynamics both affect and are affected by kinship, economic and political dynamics in ways we will understand more fully as we proceed to address these other spheres and the social and historical relations among them. But for now, we should at least note that our concepts make no *a priori* assumptions about any particular pattern of dominance to these interrelations because, as we will see in coming chapters, in any particular society at any particular time, community dynamics may be more, less or equally important to social stability and change than any of the other kinds of activity.

Community activity can reproduce the core community relationships that already exist in a society. Or, alternatively, community activity can lead to the redefinition of core community relations, thus changing the defining character of community life. In the first case we have *social stability* allowing at most evolutionary changes in community characteristics. In the second case, however, we have a *social revolution* in community relations. Community stability or change can result from cultural processes within communities, from interactions between communities, or from impositions on community relations deriving

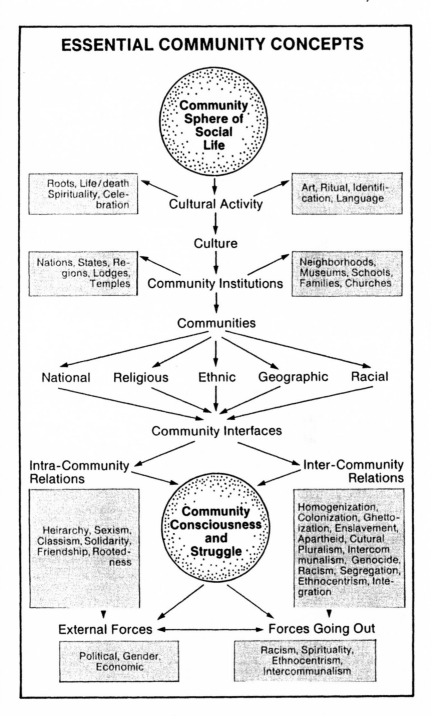

ESSENTIAL COMMUNITY CONCEPTS

Community Sphere of Social Life

Roots, Life/death Spirituality, Celebration

Art, Ritual, Identification, Language

Cultural Activity

Culture

Nations, States, Regions, Lodges, Temples

Neighborhoods, Museums, Schools, Families, Churches

Community Institutions

Communities

National   Religious   Ethnic   Geographic   Racial

Community Interfaces

Intra-Community Relations

Inter-Community Relations

Heirarchy, Sexism, Classism, Solidarity, Friendship, Rootedness

Community Consciousness and Struggle

Homogenization, Colonization, Ghettoization, Enslavement, Apartheid, Cutural Pluralism, Intercommunalism, Genocide, Racism, Segregation, Ethnocentrism, Integration

External Forces   Forces Going Out

Political, Gender, Economic

Racism, Spirituality, Ethnocentrism, Intercommunalism

from either kinship, economic or political dynamics. But even if economic, kinship and state relations are little changed by a social process that fundamentally transforms community relations—as in national independence struggles which overturn settler colonies but result in "neocolonial" economic and political orders—a social revolution has occurred. In any event, all these matters will be taken up further as we proceed in coming chapters to address other spheres of social life, societal interrelations between various spheres of social life, and the entwined historical dynamics of all of them together.

*Please Note: Readers who would now like to consider a hypothetical dialogue dealing with issues raised in chapter two should turn to page 155.

CHAPTER THREE
KINSHIP

Every society has a kinship sphere which significantly determines interactions among men, women, and children. Kinship activity revolves around sexuality, procreation, child rearing, socialization, maturation, and aging. Where community focuses on language, art, ritual, and intercommunity relations, kinship focuses on the human life cycle and interpersonal relations.

The resulting kin relations not only define sexual norms, but also how children are socialized to become adult lovers, mothers, fathers, wives, husbands, uncles, aunts and so on. The kinship sphere thus sets role requirements for participation in sexual interaction and socialization and also divides people into important gender groups, just as economic relations divide people into classes.

Kin Categories: Biological or Social Determination

It is true we are born either male or female and that biological differences alone determine who can and who cannot bear children and breast feed. But in and of itself the biological difference between being male and female determines little else. It does not determine how passive or aggressive we will be in sexual encounters. It does not determine whether we will be more attracted to members of the male or female sex. It does not determine whether we will be more proficient at "nurturing" others or at manipulating abstract concepts. It does not even alone determine one's height, weight, or density, although there are statistically significant differences between male and female averages in these areas. Nor does being male or female alone determine strength, speed or endurance, although, here too, even with other influences equal, we might find statistically significant differences in male and female averages.

33

The point is that sexual biology dictates a particular "division of labor" *in only two regards: giving birth and breast feeding.* Beyond this, it has long since become an elementary truth, at least for informed critics of entrenched oppressive relations, that *all other gender relations are socially established.* What's more, in every case where differences exist between what men and women do—including the bearing of children—*the meanings given these differences are socially defined.* But let us investigate this a bit further.

Socially-created kin categories define particular roles in the social activity of reproduction, specify gender qualifications for filling the various roles and, most important, determine the social meaning and value associated with the different roles. The social relativity of all this must be recognized. For instance, what it means to be a "father" or "mother" can differ from society to society. The kin category of "godmother" or "maternal uncle" may be important in one society but not even defined in another. Even the degree to which "blood" relations mean more or less in a society depends on the extent to which important kinship functions are carried out by "blood" or "non-blood" "relatives." If, for example, children are reared by unrelated nannies or other surrogate caretakers, biological motherhood and fatherhood may be of reduced significance from the point of view of kinship roles. What it means to be "heterosexual," "homosexual," or "bisexual"—and whether it carries any broad social significance—also varies from society to society.

How people interact with one another in kinship activity is established by the kinship institutions of the institutional boundary and the patterns developed in the human center. Every society has a kinship structure in which people engage in kinship activity and interact within the contours of families, extended families, sexual communities and sub-communities, and whatever other institutions exist in the kinship sphere. As a result, everyone identifies, in part, according to kin categories. We see ourselves as men or women (not always according to biological criteria), as having particular sexual preferences, and as being parent, child, sibling, or grandparent. Each identification affects how we view ourselves and other people and what needs and interests we develop. To the extent that kinship categories differ in different societies, the pattern of interests and needs they generate will vary as well. There is almost nothing genetic about all this.

Since no specific role pattern and no particular rule of sexual assignment is biologically determined, each society must determine roles and assignments through a social process. For this reason we can justifiably ask whether any particular set of kinship relations promotes equitable and fulfilling human socialization or whether it restricts people's ability to fulfill all that their biological potential allows. Kinship relations are not "God-given," or "nature-given," but historical. If a particular set fulfills us, we can celebrate its virtues. If a particular set oppresses us, we can struggle to change it.

Patriarchy

In spite of the many different kinds of kinship relations that have existed in different societies, there has been a remarkable continuity regarding a few important features of most kinship systems of which we have any knowledge. Since one critical kind of domination relation that has plagued human history is the domination of men over women, *patriarchy*, or male supremacy, has appeared as a key feature of most kinship systems to date.

"Patriarchy" is the name for any kinship system in which the role divisions between gender groups grant fewer duties and more benefits from kinship activity to men than women. "Sexism," refers broadly to the mindset and behavior associated with and supporting patriarchy. In the words of Adrienne Rich, quoted earlier:

> Patriarchy is the power of the fathers: a familial-social, ideological, political system in which men—by force, direct pressure, or through ritual, tradition, law and language, customs, etiquette, education, and the division of labor, determine what part women shall or shall not play, and in which the female is everywhere subsumed under the male.... Under patriarchy, I may live in *purdah* or drive a truck;...I may serve my husband his early-morning coffee within the clay walls of a Berber village or march in an academic procession; whatever my status or situation, my derived economic class, or my sexual preference, I live under the power of the fathers, and I have access only to so much of privilege or influence as the patriarchy is willing to accede to me, and only for so long as I will pay the price for male approval.[1]

Labeling a society "patriarchal" tells us that its gender relations are oppressive to women while they give power to men. Kate Millett writes:

Our society, like all other historical civilizations, is a patriarchy. The fact is evident at once if one recalls that the military, industry, technology, universities, science, political office, and finance—in short, every avenue of power within the society, including the coercive force of the police, is in male hands.[2]

But to label a society "patriarchal" is not comprehensive. The label fits most historical kinship forms, just as the label "class-divided" applies to feudal, slave, capitalist, and state-socialist economies. Calling a society "patriarchal" tells us that men dominate women, but little about the *particular* forms and mechanisms this relationship takes. To do better, we need more refined concepts to distinguish different types of patriarchy, just as the concepts "feudal" and "capitalist" distinguish different types of class divided societies. But, to date, feminists do not agree about how to make these finer distinctions and we will not attempt to do so here.

"Mothering" and "Fathering"

Patriarchal societies are characterized universally by a sexual division of labor and reward. This division has many elements of varying impact. For example, inheritance is generally man-centered, women generally take men's names when they marry, women generally do less public tasks, women's rewards in the form of wages and status are lower than men's, sexual expectations are differentiated, and so on. But most important in the analyses of many feminists is that in patriarchal societies women "mother" and men "father." Though this difference may seem obvious—of course women mother, mothers are women; of course men father, fathers are always men—the fact of the matter is that "mothering" and "fathering" are social roles that both men and women are biologically capable of fulfilling. Mothering and fathering are two aspects of "parenting" which have been divided from one another and "gender-identified" to enforce social and personality divisions that would otherwise be absent. Why men do not often mother, and why women do not often father must be explained by social and historical reasons.

In traditional terms, "mother" means the female parent. But "to mother" means to provide nurturance and to care for and care about. To mother means to see the tasks of cleaning, loving, and teaching a child as one's personal priority, and to organize one's life, in large part, around their successful accomplishment. Mothering is a fulltime job.

By equating "mother" and female, and "to mother" and a particular set of responsibilities and inclinations, our use of words says that women are by nature inclined toward certain types of (what we then label) "feminine" behaviors.

In contrast, in traditional terms, "father" means the male parent. But "to father" refers to a modest role that involves disciplining, playing, and sometimes teaching. Fathering doesn't require constant attentiveness and is not nearly so central to one's identity as mothering. One fathers a few minutes or hours a day, and frequently not for days at a time. "To father" is never more than a part time job. Identifying men with "father" and "father" with these limited responsibilities only minimally augments our understanding of what men are. This view says that men are by nature inclined toward certain types of (what we then label) "masculine" behaviors which are socially assertive and outgoing but with the nurturant element sublimated. Moreover, these divisions are communicated to children as well. As Nancy Chodorow argues in *The Reproduction of Mothering*:

> ...the contemporary reproduction of mothering...is neither a product of biology nor of intentional role training...women as mothers produce daughters with mothering capabilities and the desire to mother...[and] men whose nurturant capacities have been...suppressed. The sexual and familiar division of labor in which women mother and are more involved in interpersonal, affective relationships...produces in daughters and sons a division of psychological capacities which leads them to reproduce this...division of labor."[3]

Yet, none of this is biologically inevitable. It is perfectly possible to conceive of a society where women father and men mother, or, preferably, in which women and men both "parent." Likewise, the social status and power derived from mothering, fathering, or parenting is not inherent in the roles themselves, but results from social factors. There is nothing inconceivable about a society in which women only mother and in which men only father, maintaining a gender division of labor, but in which it is women who garner higher status and social power than men from this difference, thus reversing the order of the hierarchy.

However, as biologically feasible as the above possibilities might be, none have occurred frequently—or perhaps even at all—in the human history we know. And the discovery that females "mother" and males "father" in all known patriarchal societies is highly suggestive:

one foundation for male domination of women is probably the "binding" of women to mothering which "frees" men to focus their attention on non-household activities that are in turn awarded greater social status.

And even beyond freeing men for more valued social activities, the different psychological dynamics of mothering and fathering produce profound differences between the psychologies of men and women, and these in turn have broad implications for the ability of men and women to achieve social recognition in a patriarchal society. The personality traits corresponding to mothering and fathering become equated with what it is to be a man or a woman in a society where women mother and men father. Thus one basis for differential esteem in all social roles—not just the roles of mothering and fathering—is their relative demand for personality traits associated with mothering or fathering. It follows then, that even when mothers get out of the home they are seriously handicapped in competing for esteemed roles in patriarchal societies.

In this way the asymmetry between men's and women's parenting roles extends to the entire social division of labor. In patriarchal societies some tasks are deemed "female" and others "male." Female tasks include cleaning, tidying, cooking, serving, and certain forms of exhibitionism, which all then appear to be as deserving of low esteem as the job of wife and mother they resemble. Male tasks include making war, governing, and producing whatever are considered the more "important" economic goods in the more "serious" and "important" ways.

Women might be allowed to succeed not only as mothers and housekeepers, but also in other sexually defined roles like nurses, teachers, actresses, or models. The specific sexual division of labor may differ from society to society and generation to generation, but women-dominated fields are by definition lower-status. For example, in the United States, bank tellers and clerks had much higher status before they became female-dominated fields, with clerks transformed into secretaries. In the Soviet Union, the majority of doctors are women, but the status of the field is relatively low.

In sum, the differential human consequences of mothering and fathering and their full social extension—rather than any important biological differences between the sexes—can result in more or less differentiated male and female "modes" of existence. How we perceive and interact with the world, the kind of emotions we have and the extent to which we relate to them, and even the way we walk and talk can all come to depend on whether we adhere to the male or female "mode" of being. It follows that in order to help activists properly understand any society it is essential that among other accomplishments "liberating theory" provides concepts able to reveal the ways in which men's and women's lives differ, and, if patriarchy is present, what its implications are and how it is enforced and reproduced. And, in that light, an additional critical dimension of kinship relations and manifestations of patriarchy has to do with sexuality and sexual preference.

Homophobia and Heterosexism

Heterosexism is the oppression of gays and lesbians and the belief that heterosexuality is superior to homosexuality. Homophobia refers specifically to anger at and the dread of homosexuality, but it is also used loosely to define heterosexist behavior, subtle or overt. In *The Homosexualization of America*, Dennis Altman writes:

> It is not uncommon to hear calls for castration and even the death penalty for homosexuals among some fundamentalists...The language of homophobia is remarkable for its vehemence (why was homosexuality and not rape or murder long seen as "the unmentionable and abominable crime"?), and its frequency—Anglo-Celtic slang, in particular, is full of references to homosexuality: "cocksucker," "bugger," "pansy," "faggot," "poofter" are all common terms of abuse—is striking, as if the constant reiteration of homosexual words and references will somehow ward off the reality. Most clearly, homophobes constantly speak as if homosexuality were contagious and place great stress on "protecting" children from any contact with homosexuals: it is hard to explain logically how homosexuality can at the same time be "disgusting" and "unnatural," and yet so attractive that only the most severe sanctions will prevent its becoming rampant.[4]

In "coming out," gay men and lesbians may risk bodily harm ("gay bashing" and rape), involuntary hospitalization in a mental institution, excommunication by the church, rejection by friends and family, dismissal from the job, eviction and, since another manifestation of heterosexism is the idea that gay men and lesbians do not and should not have children, loss of custody of children. Lesbian mothers, in particular, have fought and lost many a custody battle with former male spouses. In Boston, in 1985, two gay male foster parents had their foster children removed from their care, and the Massachusetts State Legislature passed a bill that ensures that surviving partners of gay couples who have children may find they have no parental rights with the death of the biological or adoption parent, even if they have been named the legal guardian.

In the United States, homophobia and heterosexism cross all community lines. Black nationalists have variously defined homo-sexuality as a "white man's disease," a "decadent" manifestation of cultural decay, or "genocide." Cherrie Moraga writes of both sexism and heterosexism within Chicano culture and *la familia*:

> We believe the more severely we protect the sex roles within the family, the stronger we will be as a unit in opposition to the anglo threat...

> ...Living under Capitalist Patriarchy, what is true for "the man" in terms of misogyny is, to a great extent, true for the Chicano. He, too, like any other man, wants to be able to determine how, when, and with whom his women—mother, wife, and daughter—are sexual. For without male imposed social and legal control of our reproductive function, rein-forced by the Catholic Church, and the social institutional-ization of our roles as sexual and domestic servants to men, Chicanas might very freely "choose" to do otherwise, including being sexually independent *from* and/or *with* men. In fact, the forced "choice" of the gender of our sexual/love partner seems to precede the forced "choice" of the form (marriage and family) that partnership might take. The control of women begins through the institution of hetero-sexuality.[5]

Understanding the relationships that define sexuality and people's reactions to different sexual preferences is part of understanding the basic defining relations of any society. Later we will return to this issue to ask whether the concept of a "kinship sphere" provides a sufficient starting point for these necessary analyses or whether instead we need to introduce still another basic defining sphere of social life based on sexuality itself.

Radical Feminism As A Kind Of Monism

All feminists agree that the kinship sphere radiates important influences which pervade all other aspects of social life. Feminists recognize that work, politics, and cultural activity are always carried out by people who are gender-defined so that the patriarchal division of society doesn't stop at the bedroom or kitchen door. Feminists note how the differences between men and women's appointed kinship activities generate different presuppositions about who they are and what their attitudes and behaviors will be which then affect all their activity. And feminists challenge the assumption that some kinds of jobs are "naturally" suited to men and others to women, arguing that the differential rewards they receive are not simply the "natural" outcome of competitive market forces.

But "radical feminists" have gone further and transformed their insights into a sex-based monist theory in which the kinship sphere is presumed to dominate all other aspects of social life. For radical feminists, the kinship sphere becomes "base" and all else "superstructure." Patriarchal domination and gender struggle become the fundamental differentiation against which all other social differentiations must be interpreted. As Robin Morgan expressed the view:

> ...sexism is the root oppression, the one which, until and unless we uproot it, will continue to put forth the branches of racism, class hatred, ageism, competition, ecological disaster, and economic exploitation.

No other human differentiations can be similarly powerful in reproducing oppressions, and so, Morgan concludes, "women are the real Left."[6]

Shulamith Firestone summarizes the radical feminist position by paraphrasing Engels:

> [Feminist] materialism is that view...of history which seeks the ultimate cause and the great moving power of all historic events in the dialectics of sex; the division of society into two distinct biological classes for procreative reproduction; and the struggles of these classes...in changes in the modes of marriage, reproduction, and childcare...in the first division of labor based on sex...[and] in the connected development of other physically differentiated classes [castes]...which [develop] into the [economic/cultural] class system.[7]

Despite the fact that some of the sharpest insights of the feminist movement have come from radical feminism, the reductionist premise radical feminism involves is no more justified or less debilitating than the reductionist premise of cultural nationalism discussed earlier. Radical feminists underestimate the importance of other spheres of social activity and other forms of domination. They overlook the profound influence of other spheres of social life on kinship relations themselves. They often over-exaggerate the influence of kinship relations on the rest of society.

Radical feminists underestimate the extent to which a working class woman, for example, is affected by her class experience as well as her gender experience. Radical feminists also minimize the extent to which the gender experience of a working class woman is different from the gender experience of an upper class woman. Similarly, a black lesbian has both racial and gender experiences that differ substantially from those of a white lesbian. Yet all these differences are obscured by a monist feminist framework. To deal with them it is essential that feminist concepts leave room to incorporate influences from other spheres of social life.

Feminists rightly assert that history is a history of gender struggle, both because gender divisions are the basis of a primary domination relation and because gender norms permeate class, political, and cultural relations. But we have already argued that history is a history of community struggle. And we will soon see that it is equally true that history is a history of class struggle and a history of political struggle— for precisely the same reasons it is a history of gender struggle. There is nothing inconsistent in these claims. Instead, it is a myopic monist viewpoint that makes complementary insights appear incompatible and undermines the possibility of solidarity among diverse movements with different primary agendas. A rightful feminist critique of the ways that other monist approaches neglect gender can wrongly grow into dismissal of the importance of other facets of left thought and practice as, for example, in the following passage from Adrienne Rich:

> For many of us, the word "revolution" itself has become not only a dead relic of Leftism, but a key to the deadendedness of male politics: the "revolution" of a wheel which returns in the end to the same place; the "revolving door" of a politics which has "liberated" women only to use them, and only within the limits of male tolerance.[8]

To develop a workable "liberating theory" in coming chapters we must incorporate the insights of feminism into a broader conceptual framework which retains the integrity of the gender focus *and* equally highlights the impact of forces from other spheres throughout society and within kinship as well.

Conclusion

Depending on the particular pattern of kinship institutions and relations, sexual needs can be developed and molded in different ways—leading to more or less satisfaction or frustration—and children can be socialized to different patterns of adult roles through different systems of assigned duties, obligations, and prerogatives—characterized by more or less repression of their potential. So every kinship system implies not only "How does it work?" questions, but "How *well* does it work?" questions too: How well does the system develop and satisfy human sexual potentials? How little of children's initiative and creativity is repressed in the process of socialization?

It is true men are pressured to narrow their psychological development to accord with a patriarchal definition of what a "man" should be, specifically stunting nurturing capacities and ways of relating to their own emotions, other people, and even the physical universe, as they hone their "masculinity." So it is also true that patriarchy entails a loss of potential sexual and social satisfaction for all men. But as we found when examining the consequences of racism for dominant and subordinate communities, patriarchy's suppression and warping of human potentials is *not* symmetrical for men and women. As in all domination relations, although both parties are disfigured, the greatest burden of the system falls clearly on the subordinate groups— in this case women in general, the young, the old, gay men, and lesbians.

But kinship structures are not frozen in time. Kinship systems can be thought of as kinds of dissipative systems in which alterations in institutional roles and human characteristics are most often "damped," in Prigogine's sense, to remain within defining norms. Disruptive pressures can come from without, for example when a war draws more women into the work force, new economic products inundate the household with electronic gadgets, or religious upheavals lead to changes in cultural definitions that throw gender definitions into question as well. Or, pressure for change can come from within, for

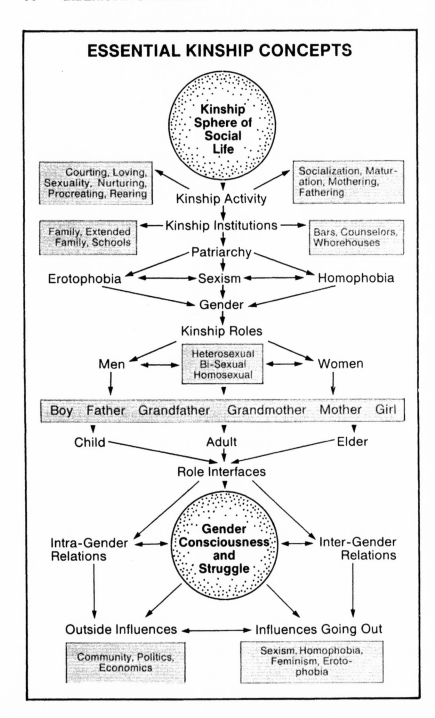

ESSENTIAL KINSHIP CONCEPTS

example when new means of birth control radically alter the consequences of sexual activities or when youth rebellion stemming from changing family patterns alters socialization processes. But these are matters we address in coming chapters on society and history.

Lastly, in comparing the kinship sphere to the community sphere—and later to economics and politics—we should recognize that each has pervasive influences on social life. Each defines critical social divisions among people. Each generates critical psychological differences between people. And each has roots in institutional and psychological aspects of society that influence one another and are influenced by other aspects of society as well. Each influences the other and is influenced by the other, and so each affects history in a complex pattern we will better understand as we proceed.

*Please Note: Readers who would now like to consider a hypothetical dialogue dealing with issues raised in chapter three should turn to page 161.

CHAPTER FOUR
ECONOMICS

To avoid incorporating biases that would prove detrimental to a complementary holist approach special care must be taken in modifying existing radical economic theory. We thus begin our analysis by presenting seven major adaptations to familiar marxist ideas.

A Summary of Innovations

Economics certainly involves the production, consumption, and allocation of material objects and activists need to understand how the transformation of "raw materials" into "intermediate" and "final" products and the distribution of those products affect material incomes. But economics also affects people as they engage in different kinds of economic activities. Our personalities, skills, consciousness, and relations with others form and transform as we repeatedly engage in economic activities. This too should be a focus of attention.

Changing a person's role in the economy—from capitalist to worker, for example—will change many of the social pressures (and benefits) that mold his/her life. Change the nature of the economic system as a whole—from feudal to capitalist, for instance—and you will change the pattern of roles and economic circumstances facing everyone. Economic activity therefore affects the qualitative human dimensions as well as the quantitative material dimensions of life. It affects social relations and people as well as things. A first priority in a complementary holist approach to economics has to be to include personality, skill, knowledge, consciousness, and different kinds of qualitative social relationships as central economic concepts.

One way of thinking about how economic activity transforms objects, people, and the relations between people is to think of that activity as "consuming" various "inputs" and "producing" a variety of "outputs." When we focus on the outputs we call the activity "production" and when we concentrate on the inputs we call the activity "consumption." In automobile production, for instance, we are concerned with the car as product. But when a person consumes a car we look at the same commodity not as the end of production activity but as the means of a kind of consumption we call travel. In other words, "production" and "consumption" are just two different views of any economic activity, since all economic activity both "consumes" inputs and "produces" outputs. Even when we travel, for example, we certainly consume fuel, the labors of airplane pilots, etc., and also produce the transport of ourselves to new locales, our changed states of mind, exhaust, and so on.

But to take the auto example further: in automobile production steel and rubber, and human energy, skills, and personality traits are all consumed as inputs, while automobiles, pollution, and exhausted workers (with certain traits either reinforced or transformed) are produced as outputs. Likewise, in automobile consumption the new car is consumed as an input and a used car is produced as an output, but the user's status in his/her neighbors' eyes—a social relationship—is also enhanced or diminished (depending on the kind of car and neighbors.)

The point is that in *both* what we call production and consumption, material, human, *and* social inputs are consumed *and* material, human, *and* social outputs are produced. For activists it is particularly critical that we incorporate in our conceptual framework means to highlight the latter human and social inputs and outputs of both production and consumption activity.

Because economic institutions define what kinds of economic activity will and will not take place, and because the economic activity we engage in affects our personality, skills, and consciousness, economic institutions profoundly affect society's social and psychological patterns as well as its material possibilities. Economic institutions also profoundly affect the needs or preferences people will develop and the productive skills they will learn. A useful set of economic concepts must therefore direct us to ask: how does market exchange influence consumer personalities and preferences? How do markets influence the structure of workplaces, and vice versa? How would central planning change consumers' or workers' roles? And what are the human effects of social relations within each workplace? A useful conceptualization must not presuppose the inevitability or neutrality of any particular set of economic institutions, but explore the particular human developmental effects of every set of economic institutions it examines.

All but the most lackluster economies can generate more material outputs than necessary to 1) replace the produced material inputs used, and 2) house, feed, and clothe those engaged in economic activity. Though the measurement of this "material surplus" or "net product" is inevitably somewhat imprecise, it is an important concept nonetheless. And a useful economic theory should identify all factors that influence the size and distribution of this net product among different classes and sectors within classes. We therefore need economic variables sensitive to how and why capitalists, professionals, managers, and workers receive different incomes; why workers earn different wages depending on their occupation, union status, race, skills, and sex; and why capitalists receive different profits depending on the kinds of competition they face and the character of their work force. It will not do to employ concepts that minimize these differences as if they had only insignificant effects.

Classes are groups of people who share sufficiently similar economic circumstances to have common interests and the potential to recognize and act on those common interests as collective agents. Many factors can help make a group a class, including sharing the same relationship of ownership or non-ownership to different types of property or holding different positions in hierarchies of power. But we must additionally highlight that qualitative factors can also help define classes whenever people do similar enough work with similar enough relations to others so they will evolve shared perspectives and desires. It isn't simply ownership, or power, or any other single factor that creates a class but a combination of factors that causes similarities in world view, interest, etc. We can't *a priori* say what all the relevant factors will be for all types of economy. We must investigate. Capitalists, for example, are a class not only because they own means of production or exert control over investment decisions, but because they share similar qualitative circumstances regarding their overall roles and relations to others in the economy.

The most important classes in any economy are those that have the potential to dominate economic decisions, appropriate the greatest part of the material surplus, and monopolize the most desirable economic roles for themselves. In other words, the most important classes in an economy are those that are already or have the potential to become a "ruling class." Marxists additionally assume that the most important ruling *group* in any society must be the ruling *class*. We reject this presumption but without rejecting the concept "ruling class" since it is perfectly possible for a class to dominate the economic sphere (making it a ruling class), yet be subordinate to another social group defined principally by political, community, or kinship characteristics. Of course it is also possible that of all the dominant groups in a society the ruling class is the most important or that group hierarchies within a society vary in importance depending on the focus of concern. But, in any case, we insist that these are matters that can only be settled by empirical investigation of particular societies. No social theory can provide us advance knowledge as to which, if any, elite will dominate the others.

In any event, once we recognize that economic activity affects personality, consciousness, and capabilities; once we recognize that control of the use of the means of production can be as critical or more critical than ownership; once we recognize that a monopoly of information can form the basis of a class's economic power just as a monopoly of ownership or a monopoly of skills can; we are able to see a new "class map" of capitalist and existing post-capitalist societies. In addition to the capitalist and working classes we see an important third "coordinator" class in modern economies.

In our view, modern economies, of both capitalist and post-capitalist varieties, have spawned a new class of managers, technocrats, and professionals who compete for control over economic activity and its benefits. Since we feel this class comes from, but is much smaller than the growing stratum of "mental workers" in modern economies we call it the coordinator class to distinguish it from the larger stratum that would include elementary school teachers as well as tenured professors, engineers of all kinds, and nurses as well as hospital administrators and doctors. In economies where the capitalist class still dominates, the coordinator class has antagonistic interests with capitalists who are their most frequent employers. Coordinators seek ever more autonomy from capitalist supervision as well as growing shares of the surplus. But in such societies the coordinator class also has antagonistic interests with the working class whose activities it largely directs and "coordinates." Coordinators seek to reproduce the dependence of workers on experts and the coordinators' own relative monopoly on expertise. In countries where private ownership of the means of production has been largely superceded by state ownership, coordinators are the only specifically economic elite, the new ruling class, but they frequently divide into two "fractions"—the local managers with their supervisory and technical staffs, and the central planners with their staffs of bureaucrats and experts—which vie with one another as well as with workers and non-economic elites for economic power.

We feel that if a "class theory" is to be useful in studying modern economies it is critical that it recognize the existence of a "coordinator class" (regardless of what name is chosen), and emphasize the importance of its interrelations with capitalists, workers, non-economic elites as well as the broader stratum of conceptual workers lodged between coordinators and workers. A class theory that hides the power of this major economic group by classifying it as the petit bourgeoisie; or a class theory that minimizes the conflicting interests of coordinators and workers by lumping coordinators into the "new working class" (or labor aristocracy), will obscure critical class relations and cause programs to serve coordinator rather than worker aims.

Lastly, a complementary holist approach to the economy emphasizes that all economies exist within societies containing other important social structures, and therefore economies are necessarily textured by "forces" emanating from other spheres. As Nancy Hartsock says, "Class distinctions in capitalist society are part of a totality, a mode of life which is structured as well by the traditions of patriarchy and white supremacy. Class distinctions in the United States affect the everyday lives of women and men, white and black and Third World people in different ways."[1]

It follows that an economy of a particular type would not function the same way if it interacted with a racist community sphere instead of a non-racist one or existed in a patriarchal setting instead of a non-patriarchal one. An example that has been more frequently debated by marxists is the difference between "parliamentary capitalism" and "fascist capitalism." But what has eluded participants in these debates is that not only are the political spheres different in "parliamentary" and "fascist" capitalism, but the "capitalist" economies differ as well. In other words, an abstract theory of "capitalist" (or coordinator) dynamics, should not be confused with concrete economic theory relevant to a particular social setting. An economic theory relevant to a racist, sexist, capitalist economy, for example, must contain concepts that "track" the effects of other "fields of force" emanating from outside the economy, but acting within it just as surely as capitalist dynamics do. In this kind of economy a "sex-blind" and "race-blind" theory of distribution of the social surplus or of job-types would also be "blind" to many important economic dynamics and forms of specifically economic oppression including the qualitative subordination of women and minorities in jobs that are not only underpaid, but whose role definition reproduces sexist and racist ideology. We need more encompassing concepts.

The Failings of Marxist Economic Theory

The points surveyed above are intended as important correctives to marxist economic theory. We take great pains to insulate our complementary holist analysis from the failings of marxism for two reasons. First, the effects of marxism on activist thought are so powerful that it influences almost all progressive theory and practice, frequently in ways of which we are unaware. Second, the failures of marxism go beyond the problem of monist exaggeration of one sphere's sway, since the economy itself is misunderstood. Before presenting the outlines of our analysis of capitalism, we summarize the major deficiencies of marxist economic theory.

As a monist economic theory marxism exaggerates the importance of economics and minimizes the importance of other spheres of social life to the point of being "economistic." This economism takes the form of underestimating the importance of non-economic forms of domination, incorrectly reducing those forms of domination to economic roots, and failing to recognize how community, gender, and political dynamics have powerful effects on economic structures. Marxists are right to emphasize the immense importance of economic dynamics and the critical role that classes have played in history. But just as with nationalism and feminism, to jump from these insights to a monist formulation is unjustifiable and debilitating.

But more than this, marxist economic theory fails to provide conceptual categories that help us discover how different kinds of economic activity have different effects on the development of human characteristics and needs. This omission not only devastates our ability to *evaluate* different economic institutions, it debilitates our ability to *analyze* some of the most important dynamics that influence social stability and change. In its fixation on the material, quantitative aspects of economic activity, marxism has largely ignored the human, qualitative aspects. Or, put differently, marxist economics has never become a theory of economic "praxis"—in fact, we do not live by or for bread alone.

Lastly, marxist class theory obscures even the existence of one of the most important classes in modern economies. Based on a monopoly of technical and organizational knowledge, a class who conceptualizes, coordinates, and oversees the economic tasks that others execute has come to vie for economic power with both the capitalist and working classes in modern economies. Despite its many other accomplishments, that it ignores this fact denies marxism even the accolade, "at least it provides a sufficient basis for understanding abstract economies."

The Capitalist Economic Sphere

In capitalism we see that there are three important classes who share unequally in the burdens and benefits of socially organized economic activity. Capitalists own the means of production, hire workers and coordinators, and appropriate a large share of the economy's net product as profits. Coordinators—including senior managers, engineers, lawyers, civil servants in various economic ministries, and high-ranking tenured university professors—monopolize valued knowledge to hold conceptual jobs at high salaries with considerable decision-making authority over their own and others' work. Coordinators receive part of the net product as high salaries and vie with capitalists over how an even larger part of the social surplus will be invested. In contrast, members of the working class sell their labor power for the best wage they can find, have little say over how their capacities will be utilized, and execute tasks conceived by others. It has not proved impossible for workers to gain part of the social surplus they alone produce. After all, many working classes have succeeded in their battles for higher than subsistence wages. But even under the most advantageous conditions workers receive, on average, a far smaller share of society's net product than capitalists and coordinators.

Moreover, not all actors in capitalist economies occupy positions within only one well-defined class. For example, between workers and coordinators there is what we call a "professional and managerial stratum" including teachers, welfare workers, nurses, technicians, and others—in short, most of the so-called "educated middle class." These folks have facets of their economic roles in common with coordinators—their high levels of schooling, and roles consisting largely of conceptual tasks. But they also have much in common with workers—the low wages they often receive and their lack of decision-making power.

In any event, everyone in capitalism participates in market exchange. As buyers everyone looks for the lowest prices they can find. And as sellers everyone searches for the highest prices available. But what the different classes buy and sell, and the degree to which they are able to influence the amounts they pay and receive, are *very* different.

Capitalists buy material inputs and labor power and sell the products the workers make to consumers in pursuit of as much profit as possible. Workers (and most coordinators) sell their labor power for a wage with which they buy their means of subsistence, seeking to improve their living conditions. To maximize profits, capitalists organize their work places and situate their companies in various markets very carefully. They try to get as much product from as little input as possible. They keep their work force disciplined and weak to keep productivity high and wages low. And they compete for position in various product markets to increase their monopoly power. Workers, coordinators, and middle strata members all seek to negotiate the highest wages they can and to buy products at the lowest possible prices. But in attempting to improve their negotiating position with their capitalist employers, coordinators and middle strata employees often try to expand their monopoly of knowledge and authority over production and exchange—largely at the expense of workers—over whom they enjoy relative advantages.

Market exchange is a matter of bargaining power. Those who have more power extort higher payments for what they sell and/or compel lower prices for what they buy. Other things being equal, the greater the degree of monopoly in an industry the higher the prices the capitalists in that industry will be able to charge. Large corporate customers are also more likely to be able to extract special pricing policies, payment schedules, or service contracts from their suppliers. Similarly, if workers negotiate as a unit, through a union, instead of individually, they can increase their bargaining power. Or if an employer cannot easily withstand a strike because competitors would steal away his customers, workers should be able to win higher wages.

Capitalists buy only their workers' labor power or ability to do work. They must then extract as much actual work as possible during the work day. This means they must structure the work process and job-promotion system in ways that cajole, entice, or coerce as much work as possible while ensuring that the work force goes home at the end of each shift disinclined to demand better working conditions or increases in pay. The coordinators and middle strata employees, of course, play an important role in this on-going contest. As organizers, directors, and supervisors of the work process, coordinators attempt to keep workers sufficiently uninformed and divided to prevent them from effectively reorganizing their work efforts and renegotiating their rewards more to their advantage. Sam Bowles and Herb Gintis point out:

> Organizing production hierarchically and fragmenting tasks divides the workers on different levels against one another and reduces the independent range of control for each. Both of these weaken the solidarity (and hence limit the group power) of workers and serve to convince them, through their day-to-day activities, of their personal incapacity to control, or even of the technical infeasibility of such control.[2]

But it is not only capitalists' power that is advanced by such structures. Coordinator interests are served as well, and directly at the expense of workers. Many factors affect bargaining power, and no simple equation determines how prices, wages, and profits will evolve in all settings. For example, in times of rising unemployment and fear of job loss, workers are less willing to take risks, but when there are tight labor markets employers are put in a position of not knowing if they will be able to find replacements. Increasing unemployment therefore "disciplines" the work force and leads to greater productivity and profits. Decreasing unemployment, on the other hand, strengthens workers and allows them to consider job actions and strikes. But what if some of the edge is taken off unemployment so the unemployed are not so desperate to take jobs and the employed not so afraid of getting a pink slip?

For example, if unemployment compensation is quickly forthcoming with a minimum of bureaucratic annoyance, and if quality public health care has rendered employment-linked medical insurance unnecessary, and if the welfare and public housing systems available to the unemployed are adequate and non-degrading, the plight of the unemployed wouldn't be so desperate. Indeed, many unemployed workers might refuse to take any available job no matter how demeaning or bid down wages in pursuit of work. And those who have jobs might not be so fearful to succumb to threats aimed at extracting "give back" concessions in contract negotiations. In such circumstances the link between unemployment, productivity, and wages would be greatly weakened.

Through this kind of analysis we can see how struggles over the "social wage"—or general level of support guaranteed all members of society through welfare, housing, food, health care and other social service programs—is a fight over the relative bargaining power of workers and capitalists as well as a "moral" question of what society is willing to guarantee its most exploited members. When the social wage strengthens workers so they cannot easily be disciplined by a dose of unemployment, capitalists naturally seek to revoke the social programs that threaten their power. By this brief description, we begin to see the efficacy of class analysis and the importance of paying attention to the interconnection of different trends and the multiplicity of factors that can affect bargaining powers.

But other important factors also influence the pattern of wages and prices. Not only do capitalists seek to enlarge profits and workers to increase wages and improve working conditions, professionals, managers, and especially coordinators also try to increase their incomes and the power they can exert over economic decisions. Sometimes professionals and managers seek to improve their circumstances by individually trying to improve their standing with employers, colluding, sometimes even against other coordinators. Other times they collectively seek to increase the status and legitimacy afforded to the possession of intellectual skills in society. Professional associations and formal accreditation systems are among the collective mechanisms managers and professionals have employed to enhance their power. Moreover, the situation of different economic actors can vary from industry to industry or region to region as unemployment rates, levels of unionization, or the plight of the unemployed vary.

Capitalist economies are giant wars in which participants try to win advantages by exerting whatever individual or collective bargaining power they can muster. Basic class relationships texture the entire battlefield with the capitalists occupying all the highest ground. But conditions vary from place to place as well, and many factors texture outcomes. Different industries have different degrees of concentration, are more or less unionized, more or less able to withstand strikes, and more or less able to threaten to pack up and move elsewhere. Likewise, different regions of a country or different sectors of a work force may have different levels of bargaining power. Unionization is an obvious factor, but skill levels and social relations rooted outside the economy are also important. For example, because of the special characteristics of the sale of labor power, the capitalist has an interest in keeping the work force weak and divided. This is accomplished by a variety of means including socially and technologically structuring the workplace to minimize worker knowledge and solidarity. In addition, if groups of workers come to a plant with hostilities rooted in relationships beyond the factory door, it will obviously benefit the capitalist to perpetuate and aggravate these hostilities so energies which might have gone to increasing worker solidarity and bargaining power will instead be focused on intra-worker competition.

And the effects of social divisions from other spheres are not limited to distribution of the material surplus. Job definitions may be influenced so a racial or sexual division of labor causes job roles to differ depending on whether slots are filled by men, women, whites, or members of oppressed communities. Therefore in a racist, sexist society the workplace will not only be fragmented along class lines, but along race and gender lines as well. Similarly, class consciousness varies depending on the mix of the four spheres in the whole social formation—a matter we will address further in later chapters. The point is that social divisions derived from other spheres have a qualitative as well as quantitative impact on the functioning of a capitalist economy.

Income distribution in capitalist economies is determined by the pattern of wages, prices, and profits. Each of these, in turn, depends on the relative bargaining strengths of particular buyers and sellers. Many factors affect these relative strengths including, as we have begun to enumerate, class division, unionization, industrial concentration, employment levels and patterns, the social wage, consumer organization and consciousness, racism, and sexism. On the qualitative side, economic roles and relationships are defined by the class structure of capitalism and by social divisions from other spheres as well. Hence people's attitudes toward how the economy functions and what kinds of alterations they would like to see are influenced by the mixture of class and non-class roles they occupy. In a particular society we can see both quantitative and qualitative trends, and postulate likely implications of particular policies. But the idea that within capitalism a few critical economic relations and simple laws of motion govern, is simply wrong. Even the most straightforward relations are always historical and subject to change.

Given all the above, it follows that we accept the marxist recognition that class struggle exists in capitalist workplaces and market arenas. We accept that capitalists compete for profits and that the capitalist economic system revolves around the accumulation process. We accept that capitalists make social and technological investment decisions in their plants and in society as a whole with an eye toward reproducing their own relative advantages. As a result, for example, they are more likely to expand society's war-making capacities than to improve living conditions for workers since building tanks enhances their international bargaining power while building livable housing for the poor would diminish their bargaining power at home. Even though both forms of investment would return profits, capitalists will certainly prefer the former.

But for us class struggle is a more complicated, tri-polar struggle in modern capitalist economies involving coordinators and a middle strata in addition to capitalists and workers. And in contrast to marxists, we see that wages, prices, and profits depend on a multiplicity of factors that determine the pattern of relative bargaining strengths between the different actors in a capitalist economy. Moreover, we highlight that the influence of other social spheres on the economy is critical because we recognize that forces emanating from outside the economy help define economic roles and influence economic decisions within it, a phenomenon we will study further in later chapters.

Our economic analysis also focuses on the qualitative aspects of economic activity—how it is that the organization of work and consumption under capitalism affects the pattern of human development and the reproduction or disruption of social relationships. The situations of traditional workers, capitalists, coordinators, and those in the middle strata are all different. As a result, a representative individual of each type, on average, has a different perspective on their economic role in society, prospects, and interests. This explains why we designate such people members of different classes.

Moreover, the interface between these groups and the patterns of consciousness that result are much more complicated than traditional marxism recognizes. For example, workers interact face-to-face far less with capitalists than with middle strata workers or coordinators. It is therefore not surprising that much of workers' hostility is directed at these intermediate groups instead of at capitalists; for example, working class antipathy for doctors, lawyers, and ideologies identified with "intellectuals." It is also important to recognize that members of the middle strata share many interests with traditional workers but frequently aspire to coordinator status; for example, teachers or nurses debating over unionizing or striking—questioning whether to behave in accord with the working class aspects of their situation or according to coordinator aspirations. Recognizing the complexity of class dynamics as well as the importance of racial and sexual dynamics at work within the economy makes all the more important the tasks of theorizing the "human," "psychological," or "qualitative" side of economic relations.

And we also must recognize that though classes are born in the organization of economic activity, class life extends beyond the factory and market. Classes develop extra-economic characteristics such as shared tastes in music, sports, restaurants, bars, clothes, etc. To recognize that class is economically rooted is not to deny that capitalists, workers, and coordinators also develop cultural, aesthetic, and even spiritual characteristics that deserve our attention as well. "Yuppies" may be thought of as a particular subset of the coordinator class. Blue and white collar workers are subsets of the working class.

The different roles assigned by a modern capitalist organization of production are not the only capitalist roles that have significant effects on how peoples' characteristics and needs develop. Markets compel actors to function individually and anti-socially, without taking account of the well-being of the producers who make what one purchases or the consumers who purchase what one produces. Markets make people competitive, individualistic in the anti-social sense of the word, and materialistic. We see the dollar-worth of everything but lose track of social relations and human costs and benefits to others.

We cannot overemphasize the importance of these facts for life in capitalist economies. Our personalities and tastes depend partially on market constraints. Markets are biased to over-supply private goods compared to public goods and, in response, we privatize ourselves to want what markets offer. Markets provide goods designed for the lowest common denominator of intelligence and interest and, in response, we brainwash ourselves to want what's to be had. And the same holds for work life. Capitalist jobs require a facility for enduring boredom and being passive and, in response, we lobotomize ourselves to deaden our capacities lest they exceed employer requirements. In both goods markets and jobs markets individuals are "free to choose" among available offerings. But what is made available is largely determined by the institutional biases of capitalism. In response, by adjusting our individual desires toward the kinds of goods and jobs capitalism is supplying and away from the kinds of goods and jobs that capitalism never offers, so we will most often have our "desires" met, we collectively help reproduce capitalism's biases. It is sensible to mold our tastes so that we want what is available rather than things we can never find on the market. Or is it? We get what we seek, yet our acts reproduce our oppressions.

Capitalist economic relations include a vast network of roles textured by class as well as race, sex, and political struggles. But when we act within the confines of those roles—as we must do if we are to gain what society has to offer—we also reproduce the defining class and other social divisions and thereby the system of privileges that benefit the socially advantaged. In other words, in addition to whatever needs we satisfy through our work and consumption activity, that activity has material and psychological effects that help reproduce capitalism.

Ironically, our ability to make the best of a bad situation also serves to reproduce our oppressive circumstances. As Herbert Marcuse put it, "What is now at stake are the needs themselves. At this stage the question is no longer: how can the individual satisfy his [or her] own needs without hurting others, but instead how can he satisfy his needs without hurting himself and without reproducing, through his aspirations and satisfactions, his dependence on an exploitative apparatus, which, in satisfying his needs, perpetuates his servitude?"[3]

Since we must eat, we work. Since we must keep our jobs, we mold our wills and capacities to fit them. To attain fulfillment through consumption, we train our tastes to what can be bought. We mold ourselves to fit the contours of our environment, thereby establishing meetable needs but also reinforcing that environment and diminishing our chances for real liberation. And we even sense the irony of what we do. As Andre Gorz describes:

> Wonder each morning how you're going to hold on till evening, each Monday how you'll make it to Saturday. Reach home without the strength to do anything but watch TV, telling yourself you'll surely die an idiot...Long to smash everything...once a day, feel sick...because you've traded your life for a living; fear that the rage mounting within you will die down in the end, that in the final analysis people are right when they say: 'ah, you can get used to anything.'[4]

Capitalist economic activity generates means of subsistence for most, access to luxuries for many, and an ever greater accumulation of means of production for a few. In the process, it also produces biases against social consumption and self-managed work and continually reproduces the class relations of capitalism as well as oppressive sex, race, and political relations based in other social spheres. While antagonistic aims fuel perpetual economic struggles over the relative well-being of different classes and social groups, most of the time the basic social relationships of capitalism remain secure.

Under certain circumstances, however, subordinate classes can escape the narrow bounds usually circumscribing class struggle and overcome dominant classes replacing old economic relationships with new ones. Just as social stability in part results from reproductive aspects of economic activity, so social change in part results from disruptive aspects of economic activity. But these are matters we will return to once we have completed our abstract survey of each of society's four spheres.

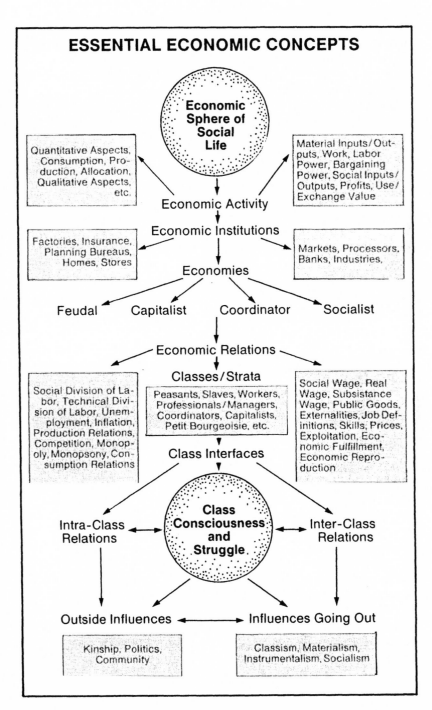

ESSENTIAL ECONOMIC CONCEPTS

Economic Sphere of Social Life

Quantitative Aspects, Consumption, Production, Allocation, Qualitative Aspects, etc.

Material Inputs/Outputs, Work, Labor Power, Bargaining Power, Social Inputs/Outputs, Profits, Use/Exchange Value

Economic Activity

Economic Institutions

Factories, Insurance, Planning Bureaus, Homes, Stores

Markets, Processors, Banks, Industries,

Economies

Feudal   Capitalist   Coordinator   Socialist

Economic Relations

Classes/Strata

Social Division of Labor, Technical Division of Labor, Unemployment, Inflation, Production Relations, Competition, Monopoly, Monopsony, Consumption Relations

Peasants, Slaves, Workers, Professionals/Managers, Coordinators, Capitalists, Petit Bourgeoisie, etc.

Social Wage, Real Wage, Subsistance Wage, Public Goods, Externalities, Job Definitions, Skills, Prices, Exploitation, Economic Fulfillment, Economic Reproduction

Class Interfaces

Class Consciousness and Struggle

Intra-Class Relations

Inter-Class Relations

Outside Influences   Influences Going Out

Kinship, Politics, Community

Classism, Materialism, Instrumentalism, Socialism

*Please Note: Readers who would now like to consider a hypothetical dialogue dealing with issues raised in chapter four should turn to page 165.

CHAPTER FIVE
POLITICS

Politics involves the creation of ideology; the setting of societal priorities, policies, laws and regulations; and the conferring of power, whether with or without majority participation and ratification. The political sphere includes the State with its military, judiciary, police, legislature, and public works; political parties; lobbying and public interest organizations, etc. Depending on the specific character of the political sphere, people may be hierarchically arrayed by electoral or appointed office, bureaucratic tenure, military rank, party position, or unofficial "backroom" influence, as well as by economic, gender, and cultural factors rooted in other spheres.[1]

People fall into different political hierarchies corresponding to different governing forms—monarchy, parliamentary or U.S.-style representative democracy, military junta, one-party dictatorship, one-person dictatorship—and variations within these governing forms. Representative democracies may differ according to such factors as size and entrenchment of the state bureaucracy, voting frequency and procedures, extent of enfranchisement, number and nature of competing political parties, and access to and control over mass communications media. Whatever form the State takes, political relations not only effect the distribution of governmental decision-making power, but also the consciousness which people bring to the economic, kinship and community spheres, and the freedom (or lack of freedom) that affects their ability to explore possibilities in these spheres. Political relations greatly affect the ways in which social institutions and structures mediate the dissemination of historical or contemporary information (and misinformation), perceive the "truth" and the "common good," and influence the parameters of public debate and individual thought itself.

Politics isn't merely a reflection of other hierarchies within a dependent unifying state. You can't understand authoritarianism in institutions and consciousness simply by extrapolating from class, gender, and community hierarchies. If the state is parliamentary, there will be one situation, but if it is dictatorial there will be another— whatever other defining features society may have. The political sphere, while it entwines with other defining spheres and feels their effects, also has *a history and set of dynamic attributes of its own* that exert defining influences back upon the rest of society. For example, if the political sphere of a particular society acts to continually repress dissent or to structurally coopt it then this certainly will have an immense impact on dynamic relations and possibilities for change in all other spheres of social life, whatever their own intrinsic attributes and contradictions may be.

Would anyone who denies this see no difference between living in a society with parliamentary democracy and one with a military dictatorship, all other social forms being otherwise "equal"? Indeed, even given that two societies have formally the same type of state, would anyone deny that great differences in the types of political movements and parties that vie for power in that society could also have dramatic impact on its citizens' quality and character of life? To understand any society, therefore, no single adjective describing a single sphere suffices.

Authoritarianism

Politics arises from the need to balance and regulate disparate aims to attain collective ends. It deals with the organization of order, and attaining order often involves the attribution of authority either to individuals or impersonal bureaucracies. But when authority is vested in unyielding, unresponsive, or irresponsible hierarchy it yields the political oppression we call "authoritarianism" by giving relatively few people excessive power at the expense of the many.

Different types of authoritarian systems impose different restraints, oppressions, and opportunities on their citizens. Authoritarian regimes need not be dictatorships. They can incorporate procedural democracy as well. Authoritarianism is rationalized in a variety of ways: ordained by God, ethnicity, gender or racial superiority, paternalism, electoral mandate, national salvation, economic efficiency, elite competence, etc.

A primary characteristic of authoritarian political relations is a drive to find a single "correct" policy or line for any particular circumstance. A plurality of proposals may be debated. But, regarding any particular problem invariably only one proposal will be given authoritative sanction as either the "divine wisdom" of a few rulers or a compromise of larger elites. The notion of the "correct line" or "common good" is an essential tool for legitimating authoritarian rule.

For example, in a U.S.-style representative democracy, decision makers gain legitimacy by asserting the need for efficiently centralizing decision-making tasks in a central authority, while promoting elected leadership as the most democratic way of balancing competing "special interests" and discerning the "national interest." Elite rhetoric focuses on the "free choice" involved in voting while obscuring the separation of all actual decision-making from the populace's will, oversight, or even awareness. There is no attention given to the fact that voters have little say in who runs for office and no power over what they do once they win office—even when elected officials ignore all campaign promises and platforms. Few would question the notion that the United States is a democracy, even though the U.S. government often does the opposite of what a majority of citizens demand; for example, a majority of U.S. citizens have been found to support the nuclear weapons freeze, national health insurance, extended environmental protection, and full employment.

In contrast, in a single party, "Soviet-style," bureaucratic dictatorship, the party claims to represent popular sentiment and to distill it through the combined wisdom of society's most intelligent and committed leaders, its Communist Party cadre. The elite party members owe their position to their coercive power and to their claim to represent the combined "scientific" wisdom of all proletarians. They tolerate criticism no more than a doctor tolerates patients criticizing a prescription.

Communication and Thought

In a dictatorship the single correct "truth" prevails because no other thought can be broached publicly without risk of repression. In a military regime or repressive party dictatorship, people are generally allowed to form only those institutions of information exchange and social debate, unions, women's organizations, and other organizations that are sanctioned by the state. Where opposition organizations exist they are subject to continual harassment and periodic wholesale repression. Voting is perfunctory or, where opposition candidates take part, fraud is used to manipulate the outcome. The media is censored directly, or indirectly through a climate of fear. Subversive thoughts can and certainly will exist, but short of revolutionary upheavals they will be kept effectively silent through fear of repression.

In countries with legal rights of freedom of speech, press, etc., and the election of political representatives, the correct line is enforced differently. Indeed, the more "democratic" governing forms a political system has, the more its channels of communication and debate must operate within parameters which reinforce the *assumptions* of elites. Since there is little control over public expression of ideas (though there is plenty of control over the resources with which to communicate those ideas e.g. access to television, university tenure, etc.), the formulation of the ideas themselves must be constrained. In other words, *what is thinkable* must be controlled so that when people manifest their rights of expression they will rarely express thoughts subversive to defining social relations. Dissidents are "red baited" or ridiculed out of the "responsible" arena of debate and policy making. Whatever their disgust with conditions in the U.S., people are more frightened of alternative images as filtered through the mass media and educational system. And in the words of E. E. Schattschneider, the "definition of alternatives is the supreme instrument of power."[2]

In the Soviet Union news commentators can and no doubt sometimes do draw the *personal conclusion* that the Soviet invasion of Afghanistan is wrong and patriotic Soviet citizens should oppose the war and support the rebels. Moreover, such a commentator might even decide to say this over public media—as indeed, one had—but, he or she would then be quickly dispatched to an asylum providing a healthy warning to others that they should keep their disturbing thoughts to themselves. In the U.S., however, although public news commentators could say almost anything on the air, risking only being fired and most often not even that, none who have large audiences and have therefore risen through the ranks of conforming pressures can even manage to think a disturbing thought. Free to speak, they have little of import to say. For example, during the period of the Vietnam War it was beyond their mental reach for any U.S. press or mainstream T.V. commentator to even think that the U.S. was the aggressor in Vietnam and that the war should not only be opposed as a mistake, but American patriots should support the Vietnamese resistance.

It follows that political systems incorporate democracy to roughly the degree that governing and other social authorities can be confident that it will be used as a form of social control—to legitimate rather than undermine their interests. Stripped of genuine participation and dissent, democracy becomes a very worthwhile system for society's elites. It allows them to argue through their disagreements about how best to pursue their own interests and to simultaneously gauge popular reactions to alternative proposals they must judge. The subversive character of democracy is diminished as subordinate groups are disenfranchised and prevented from gaining access to information and means of developing and sharing alternative ideas and programs; both these conditions operate magnificently in the U.S. And, whenever popular forces do begin to emerge in ways that can translate and transmit information and ideas widely and serve as vehicles for dominated groups to develop subversive programs, a "crisis of democracy" ensues, and there is a turn toward repression to control the situation by destroying such forms and re-engendering a passive citizenry. Keepers of the flame of democratic principle successfully reclaim their power from those who would "destroy democracy" by actually using it.

The clearest statement of the utilitarian purpose of limited or "moderate" democracy and the threat of "an excess of democracy" is found in the Trilateral Commission report, *The Crisis of Democracy*. The section on the United States was written by Samuel Huntington, the Harvard political scientist and sometime government official who praised the Vietnam War's "forced urbanization" program (designed to rid the national liberation forces of a base of popular support in the countryside). Huntington writes:

> The effective operation of a democratic political system usually requires some measure of apathy and non-involvement on the part of some individuals and groups...In itself, this marginality on the part of some groups is inherently undemocratic but it is also one of the factors which has enabled democracy to function effectively.[3]

Of course, by "some individuals and groups" Huntington means most. The "crisis of democracy," ensued in the sixties and seventies when:

> Previously passive or unorganized groups in the population, blacks, Indians, Chicanos, white ethnic groups, students, and women now embarked on concerted efforts to establish their claim to opportunities, positions, rewards, and privileges, which they had not considered themselves entitled [sic] before.[4]

As with previous periods of mass protest in the U.S., the "crisis of democracy" in the sixties and seventies was answered with a mixed program of political repression (e.g. the COINTELPRO programs) and cooptation (e.g. the anti-poverty programs). The media played a crucial role in reimposing apathy, with a constant drumbeat about the "Me Decade" of the later 1970s; a time, of course, when the anti-nuclear and gay liberation movements were, among others, on the ascent.

Anarchism as a Type of Monism

Anarchism is the name given the broad movement of people who oppose authoritarianism in all its forms. Anarchists focus their attention firstly on hierarchies directly rooted in the structure and dynamics of the state but then also extrapolate their concern for these political hierarchies to a derivative concern for other oppressions such as economic exploitation, racism, or sexism, understanding each to be a manifestation of authoritarian hierarchy in another sector of daily life. For anarchists, "hierarchy" becomes an organizing concept for all analysis as it permeates outward from the government to corrupt all aspects of life.

As a goal, some anarchists elevate the idea of individualism, extolling the ultimate freedom and isolated integrity of each separate person in society. Others favor sociality, extolling the integrity and freedom of each individual only as all are part of an integrated social whole and socially responsible for one another's circumstances and well-being. But all anarchists rightly argue that the political sphere projects forces which pervade all corners of society. The state-rooted division of society doesn't stop at the executive, legislative, or judiciary door, since the role ingrained presuppositions of people in different positions in society's political hierarchies, whatever their exact form may be, permeate all other spheres of social life. State-based hierarchies tend to reproduce all other social hierarchies by imposing them and also embodying their qualities. In Soviet-style societies, for example, the political bureaucrat, party member, and average citizen confront different circumstances and options in *all* society's institutions, not solely within the state. To rid society of any oppressions, state oppression must be overcome.

Yet, as valuable as these anarchist insights are, regrettably some anarchists overextend their valid recognitions beyond their real range of influence. They label politics the sole defining sphere of social life.

Implicitly, at least, they call the state's hierarchy society's base, the rest its superstructure. All oppressions become variants on state-based authoritarianism. They analyze racism, sexism, and classism first in terms of analyses of states and their functions, in particular power and hierarchy, not first in terms of concepts rooted in the specific dynamics of these other spheres. They may ignore other spheres entirely, or, alternatively, they may understand them, but only in the ways that they manifest specifically authoritarian relations, not in their own intricate and unique qualities. They see a hierarchy between men and women, blacks and whites, workers and bosses, and though they understand many of the emotive and material implications of such hierarchies, they fail to see all dimensions of the importance of and positive side of sexual interrelations, cultural definitions, and economic forms. They oppose marriage, religion, and complex large scale industry as necessarily statist without understanding the more complex relations associated with each of these non-government forms or the positive needs for security, continuity, spirituality and material well-being they speak to which must also be addressed in any desirable future. The liberating thrust of anarchism, therefore, sometimes succumbs to a monist narrowness which forecloses fully understanding and effectively opposing all the forms of oppression which most anarchists, in fact, do wish to overcome.

Conclusion

Change within the political sphere is most often evolutionary. Leaders come and go by election, appointment, or death. A new department of government is created. The military budget grows or shrinks. Yet, sometimes changes can grow to rupture old definitions and establish new ones. A sub-elite rises to prominence and redefines governing relationships. A military coup throws out one state elite only to install another, equally oppressive perhaps, but fundamentally different in its modes of operation.

The impetus for evolutionary and revolutionary state change can arise from within the state, owing to changes in decision-making perceptions or to conflicts between political groups, or from "without," owing to economic, kinship, or community pressures on political forms that cause their slight alteration or dissolution and redefinition. But we can only conceptualize these matters more fully in context of a broader discussion of society and history in coming chapters.

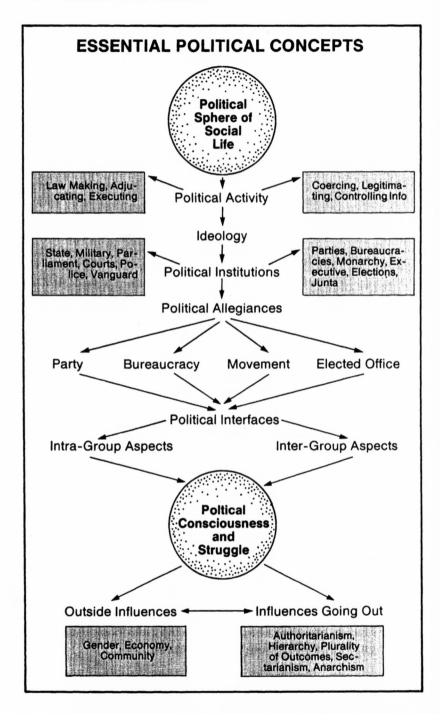

ESSENTIAL POLITICAL CONCEPTS

Political Sphere of Social Life

Law Making, Adju-cating, Executing

Political Activity

Coercing, Legitima-ting, Controlling Info

Ideology

State, Military, Par-liament, Courts, Po-lice, Vanguard

Political Institutions

Parties, Bureaucra-cies, Monarchy, Ex-ecutive, Elections, Junta

Political Allegiances

Party   Bureaucracy   Movement   Elected Office

Political Interfaces

Intra-Group Aspects   Inter-Group Aspects

Poltical Consciousness and Struggle

Outside Influences ◄──► Influences Going Out

Gender, Economy, Community

Authoritarianism, Hierarchy, Plurality of Outcomes, Sec-tarianism, Anarchism

CHAPTER SIX
SOCIETY

In chapters two to five we have shown how four spheres of social life help form the basis for important facets of daily life. To use the concepts presented in those chapters to now formulate a *monist theory* we would next have to demonstrate that one of the four spheres is more dominant than the others. For example, we might argue like cultural nationalists that community *must* exert a disproportionate influence over the forces of social stability and change because everything depends on how we culturally relate to things. Or, instead, like anarchists we might emphasize politics on the basis that the state dominates all decision-making and power hierarchies clarify all oppressions. But while to be monist we would have to highlight one sphere, as these orientations do, we could nonetheless propose any of many possible forms of asymmetry between our favored sphere and others. For example, we might argue for economic priority but urge that the economic sphere is only "determinant in the last instance" rather than always dominant. Or we could recognize the "relative autonomy of the state" *vs.* highlighted cultural differences, and so on.

Alternatively, to formulate our same concepts into a *pluralist theory*, we would need to analyze each sphere separately using "its own" concepts and then sum the results, much as many marxist-feminists do for the economy and kinship. Our key assumption would then be that the most basic defining features in each sphere are not significantly contoured by dynamics from "outside."

But in contrast to monist and pluralist approaches, if we choose a *complementary holist approach* we must anticipate the possibility of more complex interconnections between spheres even as we deny that these will always necessarily form a fixed hierarchy of influences. This approach (like socialist feminism for only two spheres) denies both the logic of elevating one sphere above others and the logic of trying to simply sum separate abstract analyses into a whole. Holism asserts that any hierarchy of influence of spheres in a particular society is something that must be empirically demonstrated in particular historical situations. It doubts that all societies even have hierarchies of influences, and it denies that the existence of a fixed hierarchy in one society demonstrates or implies the existence of the same hierarchy in another. Indeed, holism leads us to anticipate that with more exacting theories of particular societies, we will often find that all four spheres operate centrally; and this claim is based not on logical or historical necessity, but on our knowledge of conceptual possibilities and our empirical awareness.

Holism is also distinguishable from pluralism by its insistence on employing concepts from other spheres when analyzing dynamics within any particular sphere. The "summing" we advocate recognizes a greater degree of connectivity between social factors and highlights the degree to which one sphere's determining influences often help define characteristics of another sphere, so that spheres do not really exist separately, but always in the context of a whole that defines them all. Treating spheres as "networks" and "processes" that extend throughout the space of societies and the time of history is one technique for recognizing this connectivity.

Four Into One

In preceding chapters we discussed community, kinship, economic, and political dynamics as if each operated in isolation. At the same time, we have emphasized that *all human activity affects all four of these aspects of human existence.* For example, we call our activity in a factory "economic" whenever the transformation of material objects is its most important aspect for the purpose at hand. But this economic activity also has kinship, community, and political "moments." Moreover, any activity that combines material, social, and human ingredients to create material, social, and human products with new attributes is economic. But doesn't this imply that every activity has an "economic moment"? When we clean house, play, go to school, watch T.V., or attend a concert or sporting event don't we consume and produce material, human, and social factors? And, vice versa, don't work activities also socialize, create culture, and affect political options?

This recognition of the multidimensionality and essential unity of diverse activities extends to the level of the different spheres of society as well. For example, the economic sphere includes all institutions which involve production, consumption and allocation of material objects as part of their social roles. By this definition, factories, marketplaces, and banks are obviously economic institutions. But elementary schools, which we usually think of as kinship institutions because of their socialization function, also involve production and consumption of material objects, as do theaters, households, senates, churches, and ball parks. In fact, if we extend the economic sphere to its fullest dimensions, we discover that it encompasses all of society and that every institution resides within the economic institutional network. Indeed, it is this reality which makes effective theories of the economy powerful tools for understanding at least some things about all sides of social life.

But the same reasoning applies to the community, kinship, and governing spheres. Every institution has a socialization aspect, cultural aspect, and decision-making aspect as well as an economic aspect. Families historically have acted as the central kinship institution, but socialization takes place in factories, offices, and marketplaces as well. The state is the principal focus of political activity, but it also produces and consumes material objects and reproduces and transforms cultural attitudes and relations. And, as with economics, the fact that the extension of the kinship, community, and political spheres of life encompass all of society is what makes compelling theories of *each* of these spheres powerful tools for understanding at least certain things about *all* social relationships.

The four spheres share the same space and time even though they have different central institutions and focus on different social functions. It is as if societies have four centers from which four different force fields emerge, mingle, and finally merge. Each of the four force fields not only affects like options and activities throughout society, they all also affect one another, a complication that makes it difficult to comprehend the full character even of society's individual spheres. If we only study the characteristics of each field in isolation, we not only have no guide as to how to combine the results, we also mis-specify the dynamics within each field because we do not see how they are influenced by forces emerging from the other three.

The Concept of a "Social Moment"

We have said that we can think of any social act in terms of four "moments" related to the four defining types of social interaction. It is a little like the way we learned how to graphically track projectiles in high school. If we imagine a ball flying through the air we can track its path by noting at each instant how high it is, how far it has gone along our line of sight, and how far it has gone perpendicular to the line of sight. We study the forces pushing or impeding it in each of these three directions. If we want to study the ball being thrown across a field, we should choose a vertical axis in line with gravity and two horizontal axes measuring off the field in a grid along the line the wind is blowing and/or in the direction we will throw the ball. If we're tracking an airplane, we'll use longitude, latitude, and altitude. If we're tracking a spaceship, we may choose more complex "curvilinear coordinates" because in this instance they will be easiest to use.

But what if we want to track "social trajectories"? We have proposed conceptualizing society by carving it into components of four types of social relations. Yet, unlike spatial directions, these social dimensions are not linear and they do not operate independently of one another. Influences relating to each have effects on the three others. In the throwing example, gravity acting along up-down direction doesn't significantly change the wind effect along the horizontal direction. Nor does our energy of throwing across the field affect gravity's influence perpendicular to it. But in societies, changes in "forces" acting primarily along the kinship dimension influence not only gender but also economic, community, and political phenomena. In societies, *everything is mutually interactive*, and this severely complicates matters.

Yet, despite this critical complication, we choose our "social dimensions" for the same reason a physicist chooses a particular spatial conceptualization or any analyst chooses a particular way of organizing his or her concepts: to provide the most effective framework for understanding chosen subject matter in ways relevant to particular ends being sought. In choosing four social spheres, we seek enough axes to span all the social dynamics we are interested in, but, at the same time, we do not want any more axes than necessary. Moreover, for utility we want our social axes to provide maximum ease of use to activist analysts.

But what precisely do we mean by a "social moment"? Every social interaction—whether assembling cars or struggling for rent control—has aspects that can be most effectively understood through each of the four spheres we have discussed. We call these its economic, kinship, community, and political "moments" of definition. In real life, of course, these characteristics intertwine, so the four chosen social moments do not manifest themselves *separately* any more than a ball simultaneously moves along all the infinity of spatial axes we can

EACH TYPE OF SOCIAL ACTIVITY EMBODIES
MOMENTS OF ALL THREE OTHER TYPES

Kinship Moment

Governing Moment

Party allegiances evolved
Political attitudes set
Ideologies discussed
Info consumed
Info produced
Decisions made
Authoritarian values set
Attitudes to info developed

Kinship Activity

Loving   Aging   Sharing
Nurturing   Learning
Procreating   Courting
Sex   Maturing
Teaching   Socializing

Community Moment

Religious training,
Values development,
Ethnic identification,
Racial attitudes,
Moral training,
Habits passed on,
Celebrations,
Community Acculturation,

Economic Moment

Producing class consciousness
Producing labor power
Producing cleanliness
Producing personality
Allocating income
Allocating labor
Consuming goods
Consuming services
Consuming class consciousness

conceptualize. Yet gravity and wind *do* operate along specific spatial axes and so too do specific forces within society operate along specific "social dimensions." If we choose our social dimensions as those via which the most important forces most often operate, specific "social moments" will help us easily perceive the action of critically important forces and their interconnections.

One Into Four

What possible kinds of relations can exist between the four spheres and their fields of force? People aren't economically-affected in one part of their lives and gender-affected in another; state-influenced one day of the week and community-influenced some other day. Instead, they simultaneously experience economic, kinship, governance, and community involvements, and this guarantees that spheres interact. At a particular time class may have more influence on molding a person's consciousness and behavior than gender, or vice-versa. But these influences must co-exist.

Societies consist of diverse relations combined in complex ways. If the different relations became completely estranged, society itself would become impossible. Different parts of our lives would produce such profoundly contradictory thought and behavior patterns that we would become hopelessly disoriented. In stable societies, there is a constant interplay of mechanisms to reconcile contradictory dynamics before they get out of hand. Profound schisms which cannot be reconciled characterize unstable societies ripe for social revolutions. Conservative "functionalist" social theories assume that in all societies sufficient mechanisms exist to reconcile all contradictory role requirements and socialize people to accept those roles without questioning the humanity of this "fit." Radicals, on the other hand, tend to underestimate the influence of stabilizing, ameliorating mechanisms.

For example, with no interconnections, our kinship life might socialize us to become non-acquisitive and anti-competitive, while our economic life might require opposite traits. Or our community life might produce mutual respect for different cultures, while our political institutions require instrumentalist, elitist, authoritarian attitudes. If one part of society says we should have a particular quality, and another part says we should have the opposite quality, where the quality in question is one that will help define our personality and structure our life prospects, social instability arises. With no way to alleviate the resulting tensions, not only would social cohesion disintegrate as people clashed with each other, but each person's internal psychology would tend to "disintegrate" due to confused self-definition. Society would be terminally schizoid. Something would "have to give" but theory would not tell us in advance of analyzing specific circumstances what that something would be. Theory without investigation, that is, could not tell us that one of the tendencies would always dominate another. Nor could theory allow us to predict, without seeking evidence, whether the unstable situation would revert back to a former stable status quo or move on to a new social formation not characterized by dynamics that produce both qualities and their opposites. But it is precisely our theoretical knowledge of the existence of diverse types of interactive dynamics between spheres and fields coupled with detailed surveys of the conditions of actual societal relations that can together help us predict how instabilities are likely to resolve to recreate workable social orders of one kind or another. In workable social orders it follows that there will be intricate interconnections between defining spheres of social activity. In our effort to understand societies as they appear at a given moment what remains is to ask what forms these expected interconnections can take.

Accommodation

One kind of interaction between spheres that is consistent with stability is *accommodation*. Critical features of each sphere may accommodate to requirements of other spheres. For example, the assignment of people to economic roles may accommodate with a society's sexist gender and racist community hierarchies so that economic activity places men in positions above women and whites in positions above blacks. Similarly, if there are accommodation relations between the kinship and political spheres, the family will socialize children in ways consistent with the state-related roles they will play as adults and political activity will produce traits that comply with the family roles men and women are to play. In the journey from the simplest pluralism to complementary holism, recognizing "accommodation" between spheres is the first tentative step.

Co-Definition

But another more deeply "connective" type of relationship consistent with social stability is what we call *co-definition*: the different spheres "co-define" one another's internal roles and relations. For example, instead of economic roles being determined entirely by class divisions and bargaining relationships and individuals' assignments to various economic roles merely accommodating to non-economic, external hierarchies, the *very definition* of economic roles in the first place could reflect influences from kinship, political, or community spheres. Work roles in the corporation might incorporate a sexual division of labor inexplicable in solely economic terms, yet easily understood as a manifestation of a sexist field of force. Nurturing roles in the family might vary depending upon community affiliations thereby showing defining characteristics inexplicable in solely kinship terms yet easily understood as a manifestation of a cultural field of force. It would not be enough to theorize the economy and then note—via the principle of accommodation—that since men and women are differentiated by kinship relations outside the economy, they will be treated differently within the economy as well. Instead, even in theorizing the most basic elements of the economy we would have to determine the defining impact of kinship forces. And likewise for theorizing kinship and incorporating community recognitions. Recognizing this necessity is the critical step from even the most complex pluralism to complementary holism. It corresponds to the difference between those who pluralistically join orientations, like marxist-feminists, and those who holistically develop a more encompassing framework, like socialist feminists, or, taking all four spheres into account, complementary holists.

There is nothing inherent in capitalist economic relations that requires the activity of coffee-making to be assigned to the role of secretary. There is no purely economic reason why in the U.S., women are ghettoized into so-called "pink collar" jobs: clerical work, nursing, domestic work, restaurant and food service, retail sales, elementary school teaching, etc. There is nothing about economics that requires that in addition to different levels of compensation, women's and men's activities must or even should involve different degrees of oversight and mobility. Purely economic dynamics cannot explain such profound gender differentiations. In this sense, then, not only do economic relations accommodate kinship hierarchies, by placing women in the lowest "economically-defined" positions, but patriarchy "co-defines" basic economic relations.

In the very definition of economic roles only class factors can be at play—in which case, low-level, but genderless jobs will, by accommodation, go to women and others at the bottom of non-class hierarchies—or, alternatively, co-defining kinship forces can also operate so as to generate subordinate "feminine" gender-defined jobs, such as being a secretary whose responsibilities include maternal services such

"SELECTING" THE ECONOMY OF A PARTICULAR REAL SOCIETY

**Many Possible
Economies**

Feudal
Capitalist
Coordinator
Socialist

**One Specific
Economy**

Capitalism
  Specific
  Size
  Classes
  Industries
  Unions
  etc.

**Accommodating
Other Spheres**

Minorities & Women
"Last Hired, First Fired"
Labor Laws
Racist/Sexist
Income Distribution
etc.

**Co-Defining
Other Spheres**

Sexual, Racial, Political
  Divisions of Labor
  Role Definitions
  Institutional Norms
  etc.

as coffee-making, gift purchasing and birthday reminding.

Whenever gender dynamics co-define economic relations, not only will men and women be assigned to different economic roles, but those roles themselves will have characteristics in part determined by kinship dynamics. Similarly, whenever community forces co-define kinship relations, cultural differences will permeate gender roles, so families whose members belong to different communities will have different role structures. The roles of mother and father may differ significantly in Afro-American, Chicano, and Anglo-American families. The logic carries from sphere to sphere. When we look at societies via any monist theory, most dimensions of differences among people are reduced to peripheral concern. When we switch to pluralism, we see each type of difference, but not how they contour one another. When we choose complementary holism we have the potential of developing a comprehensive picture. Indeed, an especially critical consequence of co-definition that only a holist approach fully highlights is that "class consciousness" will vary depending on gender, political, and community allegiances; "womens' consciousness" will differ for women of different classes, political allegiances, and communities; "Afro-American, Latino, or Native-American consciousness" will differ depending on gender, political, and class allegiances; and "political consciousness" will vary depending upon gender, community, and class allegiances.

In short, "complementary holism" highlights all the critical kinds of possible interconnections in human societies. First, society is viewed as a whole, a single system of people and institutions inextricably bound together. Only then, and only for specific purposes, do we abstract four different component parts, or social spheres, for separate analysis. But the characteristics of each sphere are viewed as multiply determined by one another, and the specific ways in which the spheres accommodate to and co-define one another are a primary subject of examination. Still, even this array of concepts leaves us feeling insufficiently prepared. It would be nice to also focus specifically on general relations between people and what we often call "the system."

Center and Boundary

Within marxism the concepts "base" and "superstructure" play an important role. Since marxists see the economy as more important than other spheres, it is only sensible for them to carve up society according to a materialist economic hierarchy. Economic relations form the base, everything else is more or less lumped together in a dependent superstructure. Different marxists use this ordering in different ways,

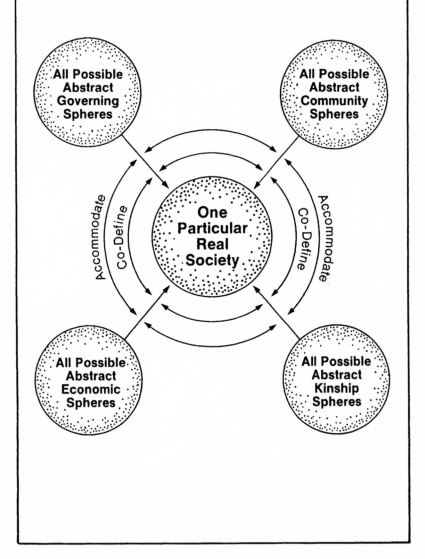

some allowing the superstructure to have more influence on the base and some less. For instance, the Maoist theory of the "Cultural Revolution" grants greater influence to "superstructural" phenomena. Feminists, nationalists, and anarchists could all also employ the "base/superstructure" terminology, although the composition of the base would differ for each.

In contrast, having located not only economics but also politics, community, and kinship in society's core, we do not want to impose a "productivist" or sphere-centering hierarchy on our method. Similarly, after having argued that material, social, and ideological relations operate interactively in each type of activity and social sphere, again we would be foolish to assert an always operative material or ideological dominance.

So while no "base/superstructure" hierarchy is compatible with a complementary holist approach, it does make sense for us to distinguish between the people in any society—with all their individual and group traits—or what we call the "human center," and the social roles, institutions, and institutional relations in that society, or what we call the "institutional boundary." The allusion to architecture in these labels has a purpose. The institutional "boundary" of a society textures possibilities by imposing systemic or structural limits on people's behavior "from without." Within any society the boundary includes the intricate array of role offerings that constitute the society's many institutions. The roles "surround" us and restrict our choices. To gain whatever benefits society has to offer—as workers, parents, voters, neighbors, etc.—we must fit ourselves into these role structures or risk being ostracized socially and penalized economically and politically. The "human center," on the other hand, embraces human feeling, need, thought, skill, consciousness, desire, creative expression, and personality. The ideas and actions of individuals and groups within the center "radiate outward" in turn influencing the boundary and even transcending successive generations.

The idea of one realm surrounding another is only a graphic approximation of the dynamic between the two realms--it is not a literal description. In fact, the center and boundary occupy the same time and space as one another and are therefore really a single whole, just as the four spheres are. And, again like the four spheres, the center and boundary also intersect, overlap, accommodate, and co-define in a complementary way. But while the spheres distinguish between different kinds of activities while lumping together the people and institutions that determine these activities, the concepts of societal center and boundary distinguish between people and institutions while lumping together different kinds of activity. Indeed, each sphere has a center element and a boundary element—people and institutional roles. Moreover, society's center and boundary each have aspects of all four spheres. The conceptual carvings are simply two compatible over-lapping ways of looking at things.

Core Characteristics

The introduction of this new set of concepts is not a matter of "different strokes for different folks," but different conceptual tools for different analytical tasks. And the next addition to our tool kit, for the task of focusing on critical defining aspects of social life, is the concept, "core characteristic." We define a core characteristic as a defining feature of a society which centrally influences life options by signifi-cantly affecting the character of both the human center and institutional boundary. Core characteristics usually begin as defining characteristics of the activity of a particular social sphere, and then, through accommodation and co-definition, come to affect the quality of life throughout the rest of society as well.

For example, in "class societies," class relations certainly help define all economic role structures and texture all economic possibilities. Yet, in addition, beyond the economy, class hierarchies usually impose themselves on the character of governing, kinship, and community relations as well. Indeed, it is because "class" frequently permeates all social definitions and textures all aspects of lived experience that the marxist label "class society" truly does have meaning beyond the economic sphere. In such situations a specific class structure will become a core characteristic affecting all of social life. In the United States, for example, capitalist exploitation is a core characteristic.

But in the United States the same holds true for sexism (flowing from the kinship sphere), racism (flowing from the community sphere), and a particular type of authoritarianism (flowing from the political sphere). In other words, not only is capitalist exploitation a core characteristic of U.S. society, but so are racism, sexism, and authoritar-ianism. While we believe this to be true for the United States, we are not arguing that in all societies at all times each sphere of social activity must generate a feature that becomes a core characteristic. Whether or not this occurs depends on the nature of the social activity in different social spheres and the nature of the interconnections between those spheres in each particular society. The important point is that multiple core characteristics are a possibility deserving serious investigation. Unfortunately, this is rarely contemplated as a possibility by most social theoreticians.

Selecting Appropriate Concepts:
Do Four Critical Spheres Suffice?

At this point, we want to address a question that is likely disturbing at least a few of our readers. We know society can be conceptualized in many different ways. We agree that the task is to formulate those conceptualizations that will most effectively meet our needs as students and agents of social change. But why choose exactly four spheres for our conceptual framework?

"Carving" societies into our four chosen spheres is only one of countless possible options. We cannot possibly maintain it provides the only effective, right, or revealing way to view things. Our argument in favor of choosing these four particular spheres to ground our theory of social stability and change rests on the validity of the following claims: 1) Each activity necessarily exists in any society. 2) Each activity is carried out through elaborate social relationships that define a significant portion of people's life prospects. 3) None of the four types of activity reduces to or is subsumed by any of the others. 4) All of the activities and spheres influence one another and all social outcomes. So, 5) if our priority is understanding society in order to change it, not highlighting any of these spheres would cause us to run a grave risk of incompletely theorizing our circumstances. And 6) if we seek the most manageable framework for developing analyses, vision, and strategy, adding additional spheres would simply complicate matters at no great gain in facilitating understanding. Of course we cannot deny the possibility that some other type of activity will meet the first four criteria so that points "5" and "6" will apply only to an expanded set of five or more spheres, but, so far, we have not found this to be the case.

Economic, political, kinship, and community relations will always exist, though their influence in different societies may vary greatly. Wherever movements seek to overcome forms of domination, we can safely bet that conceptualizing along these particular social dimensions will significantly inform their efforts. To be sure, in different times and societies, different spheres may have greater or lesser influence in defining oppressions and eliciting social movements. But lack of conscious social movement along a particular axis does not diminish the theoretical usefulness of that axis; instead, the lack of social movement itself requires explanation using the theoretical tools pertaining to the particular sphere and to others as well.

To "abstract" means to pull a part out from the whole for separate analysis. When we discuss a society's economy without paying attention to its culture, for example, we abstract out the economy from the whole. Sometimes abstractions lead to the definition of concepts and angles of focus that provide exceptional insights, not only pedagog- ically—by making our thought simpler because unessential complex- ities have been left out—but also practically, by yielding results which seem fully applicable in real societies and which would not have been seen but for making the abstraction in the first place. Other times, however, we separately conceptualize and analyze some part of a whole at great length, only to find that in real world interactions few of our abstract results remain valid.

The real world is characterized by interconnectedness. Everything exists in one whole, defined by and defining everything else. Yet within this whole, we can distinguish parts which exhibit modeled abstract dynamics which differ little from their real dynamics in complex environs. Their interconnectedness or "connectivity" with other relations doesn't intrude on the features we focus on when we consider them abstractly, isolated from interactions, at least to the degree of description we are pursuing.

The effects of quantum dynamics within falling apples on their gravitational attraction to the earth are so minute that *if* we are only concerned about the apple's rate of fall we can ignore them. In contrast, marxist, feminist, nationalist, and anarchist theories, which are gener- ally developed by abstracting economic, gender, community, and state relations from all others, end up suggesting effects which are so modified by the process of abstracting that when we take into account factors ignored in the abstract analyses, we see that those analyses are no longer reliable guides to real relations.

The point of our complementary holist framework is to provide an over-arching conceptual "carving" that can simultaneously give us an encompassing view and also refine each particular angle of conceptual- ization so it does not suffer from being too abstracted from all other angles of conceptualization. So, regarding the possible demarcation of a fifth sphere, at the conceptual level we must ask whether it clarifies or obscures our analytical vision. Radical activists must ask whether adding an additional sphere highlighting another dimension, currently subsumed in one or more or our four, would allow us to more easily see important relations for issues of social change and strategy that might otherwise have been overlooked or misunderstood. If yes, then as activists we should take this extra conceptual step. If not, it would complicate matters unnecessarily.

For example, the kinship sphere is the primary site of what we have termed kinship-sexual-child rearing activity and the principal source of divisions along "gender" lines. We have argued that division by sexual preference forms an integral part of the dynamic of kinship activity, and that just as sexism emerges from the dynamics of kinship, so does heterosexism and homophobia. Seeing things this way, we would discuss questions of sexuality and sexual preference as one complex part of the whole range of phenomena associated with kinship. This is not, however, the only approach we could take. Instead of four defining spheres, we might choose to demarcate five.

We could argue, for example, that sexuality itself is the locus of a sphere of human activity which can project defining social characteristics as autonomously as any other defining activity can. We could argue further that a basic, oppressive dynamic associated with this additional sphere of social life is "erotophobia" (the fear and hatred of sexuality) whose primary manifestation is homophobia.

The choice between these alternative frameworks depends largely on an assessment of the value of the alternative ways of conceptualizing in light of our goal of promoting social change. In a homophobic/erotophobic society, will a fourfold division that subsumes complex issues of sexuality within a sphere primarily concerned with gender produce an understanding of sexuality sufficient to our needs? Or, alternatively, just as we find it necessary to break out politics from economics, for example, must we break out sexuality from kinship—disentangling sexuality to permit a closer, potentially more insightful reading of society?

It seems evident that like economic, political, cultural, and gender activity, sexual activity has historical universality. Moreover, sexual activity often has the effect of demarcating important social divisions. But this isn't enough, since one could say the same thing about subparts of the economic sphere arguing the need to separate production from consumption and allocation, but be rebutted because this step is unwarranted due to the fact that production, consumption, and allocation are just different phases of one process that produces a seamless web of effects. Does the same hold for sexuality as an element of kinship relations? Or, with sexuality, as opposed to matters of gender definition and child rearing, do we need to employ two conceptual structures and locuses of focus to achieve full understanding?

STEPS TOWARD UNDERSTANDING
ANY SOCIETY

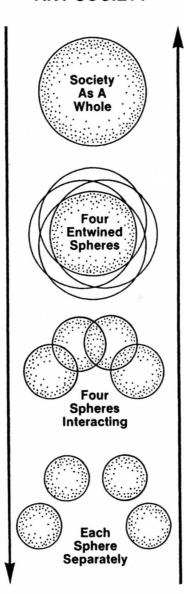

Analyze
From
The
Whole
To
The
Abstract
Elements

Society
As A
Whole

Four
Entwined
Spheres

Four
Spheres
Interacting

Each
Sphere
Separately

Analyze
From
The
Abstract
Elements
To
The
Whole

Following a similar tack an argument could be made for dividing race and religion off from ethnicity or even for including entirely new spheres of different sorts having to do, for example, with cognition/psychology. What is to prevent this? Are there times when it would be important to undertake such a step?

In chapter one we suggested a utilitarian norm for governing how we define concepts. The issue is not a matter of "abstract theoretical power" but one of "use value" in finding truths we need to understand. The point of our presenting provocative examples for possible fifth spheres has been to show that the conceptualizations elaborated in this book in no sense constitute a closed and inviolable system. But for now we think we can manage with four main conceptual angles not because we think issues such as sexuality are relatively unimportant, but because we think that like many other important dynamics, they can be effectively handled within a fourfold orientation. Whether this choice is optimal will depend on how powerful our emerging theory proves to be as we proceed to discussions of whole societies and history, vision and strategy.

A Holistic Approach To Understanding Societies

A holistic analysis of a society's school system, to take one example, would look at not only how the schools socialize children to become adults, but also how the schools pass on cultural awareness, teach necessary economic skills, and carry out political functions. A holistic analysis would identify the aspects of the socialization process in schools that reproduce society's defining kinship norms—say sexism and heterosexism—but would also identify ways in which school activities were incompatible with established kinship norms—equal budgets for male and female athletic programs or boys taking home economics classes and girls taking shop. A holistic analysis would also look for reproductive and destabilizing effects of schools on racial, religious, class, and political relations. Are children segregated and "tracked" by race, or is integration through busing or other means challenging racist norms? Are children being tracked in ways that teach conceptual skills to a few future coordinators and rote vocational skills to many, or are more children of working class parents receiving pre-college and college education than will be able to find "thinking" jobs in the economy? Are children getting a sanitized, anglicized version of American history or are they taking Social Studies courses that study the genocidal treatment of Native Americans and approach the Vietnam War from a critical perspective?

But as powerful as this orientation may be, the complementary holist approach as described so far is still incomplete. Not only have we left the fundamental issues of social stability and change to the next chapter, but, in addition we have left out all reference to the ecology and paid little attention to a world system of many societies.

The Ecological Context

The "natural ecology" includes the flora, fauna, resources, and general habitat of the non-human-created environment. It operates as an immensely complicated system in which intricate interconnections between the life cycles of different species, the climate, and the physical environment determine over-arching characteristics. A "society" includes the human created network of social relations we have spent this chapter conceptualizing. A "social ecology," however, is the combination of a natural ecology and a society which, once again, form a single complementary whole.

We can view the natural ecology and society in much the same way we have viewed different spheres within any particular society. Each shapes and is shaped by the other. Looked at from one perspective they weave a single, seamless whole. Looked at from another perspective, they act as two different systems accommodating or co-defining one another. Each perspective is useful for particular purposes and together they comprise the complementary holist view we have developed throughout this book.

For some purposes we can therefore usefully treat a society as a separate system. For other purposes, we do so at risk. For example, as the ecologists have tried to teach us, if we wish to create a world in which we can live safely for longer than another half century we can leave out ecological considerations only at our own peril. Murray Bookchin conveys this lesson, for example, when he urges that we should not allow ourselves to succumb to a heavy-handed dualism that separates the natural from the social, or to fall into a reductionism that dissolves the one in the other since committing either of these errors cripples our ability to think out the real issues involved.

Similarly, we feel that an ecological perspective needs to become part of our guiding philosophy of life. In this book we have so far included chapters on four spheres of social life and in this chapter we have argued for a conceptual approach to amalgamating the four sets of critical concepts into a holistic view of society. In addition, however, a fully complementary holist view of social ecologies sufficient to the needs of activists concerned with creating a better world also requires ecological concepts that can operate on their own and be integrated into the overall approach as well.

Yet not all ecological perspectives are equally likely to contribute to improving social or even ecological relations. For example, traditional western mainstream ecologists apply instrumentalist approaches common in modern hierarchical societies to the problem of manipulating and taming nature. These "technocratic ecologists" treat nature as another tool particular human elites can manipulate for their own ends. This view calls itself ecological, but it has nothing in common with the complementary holist approach we have celebrated. Instead this attitude toward nature co-reproduces tendencies that emerge from contemporary social forms characterized by domination and exploitation. We need to incorporate an ecological perspective that will co-reproduce a liberatory world-view.

We are confident complementary holist methodology will complement an ecologically sound attitude to the natural ecology. With Bookchin we believe that this approach can sensitize us to the intricate connection between human and non-human relationships, "neither mechanically reducing them to a false undifferentiated oneness, nor totally breaking the bonds between them to wrongly imply they are unconnected."[8] We have no doubt many "ecological concepts" will be needed in addition to the "social concepts" presented in this volume, and though we cannot discuss specific ecological concepts here, we believe they can be integrated effectively into a holist framework.

The World Context

Every society interacts not only with nature but also with other societies. Throughout history, varying forms of imperialism, national chauvinism, and strategic alliances have existed as critical factors, shaping not only the history of the world but the development of individual societies as well. Colonialism has dramatically shaped the societies of the colonial powers as well as the colonies, with the latter, of course, suffering far more damaging consequences. Countries with highly valued resources such as oil have seen their national incomes rise to dwarf countries with no such resources. Almost all societies divert enormous resources to military establishments in the face of real or exaggerated external threats. Countries perceived to have pivotal roles in geostrategic superpower competition are subject to far more consistent external pressure than less "important" countries. Intervention clearly constrains and threatens liberatory developments in

ESSENTIAL CONCEPTS FOR UNDERSTANDING ANY SOCIETY

| Kinship Concepts | Economic Concepts | Community Concepts | Political Concepts |

Social Movement   Social Interaction

Accommodation   Co-Definition

Social Field of Force

Society's Center   Society's Boundary

Core Characteristics

Ecological Characteristics

Natural Ecology   Social Ecology

Inter-Social Concepts

Imperialism   International System

countries such as Nicaragua or El Salvador. We should never forget that
intervention to destroy progressive movements and governments is the
rule not the exception, and that historically most of these interventions
have succeeded. Where revolutions have survived, they have been
distorted. Imagine how different national and world history would be
only over the last three decades if the people of Guatemala and the
Dominican Republic and Brazil and Chile and Jamaica and Grenada and
Cuba and Nicaragua and El Salvador and Vietnam and Cambodia and
South Korea and Ireland and Hungary and Czechoslovakia and Iran
and Angola and Mozambique and Zimbabwe...were able to have made
and keep making their own history without intervention by the United
States or the Soviet Union. (If the list of countries tormented by the
U.S. is longer, it's because in fact it is longer.)

We have not attempted to offer a detailed treatment of international
dynamics. But, we feel the holist approach is well suited to doing so.
Imperialism is one of the subjects most conducive to a holist analysis
since imperialism so clearly manifests all four "moments" of causation.
In our opinion, much that has been lacking in various theories of
international relations stems from ignoring one or more moments—for
example, the influence of patriarchy has been almost universally overlooked until recently—or from assuming that one or another moment
must always be dominant. Marxist-Leninist theories of imperialism
defined solely as the monopoly stage of capitalism (an economic
system) are a prime example of the latter point.

Applying a holist approach to relations between countries should
give us a better understanding of the impact of community dynamics of
race and religion, for example (e.g. in the U.S. occupation of Grenada
or British-occupied Northern Ireland or the Israeli-occupied West
Bank). It would help us understand the exploitation of women by
multinational corporations or military institutions (e.g. the use of rape
in warfare and the cultivation of prostitution around U.S. military
bases) and the role these play both in structuring the form of
international relations and their motivations. Likewise this approach
should help explicate the meaning of "cultural imperialism" (e.g. the
Westernization/Americanization of consumption and definitions of
beauty) and the role this plays.

If it turns out we need additional concepts specially suited to the
macro context of inter-society connections to get an analysis comprehensive enough for our activist needs, (as we likely need additional
ecological concepts, for example), this should not be a problem for the
holist framework. If these additions cause us to have to return to our

society-level concepts to adapt their basic definitions in light of the defining impact of world-level "fields of force," a degree of alteration we do not expect to have to undertake, that too would be a workable step for our methodology though it might lead to significant alterations to the results obtained so far in this volume.

*Please Note: Readers who would now like to consider a hypothetical dialogue dealing with issues raised in chapter six should turn to page 173.

CHAPTER SEVEN
HISTORY AND SOCIAL CHANGE

Can we ever understand history? Can we explain this long-running drama, with its countless plots and subplots—past, present and future? Or can we only provide narrow post-mortems of brief interludes? Can we conceptualize social change in ways which enhance strategy and program? Frederick Engels, one of science's great popularizers, described history's imponderability this way:

> When we consider and reflect upon Nature at large or the history of humankind or our own intellectual activity, at first we see the picture of an endless entanglement of relations and reactions, permutations and combinations, in which nothing remains what, where, and as it was, but everything moves, changes, comes into being and passes away. We see therefore at first the picture as a whole with its individual parts still more or less kept in the background, we observe the movements, transitions, connections, rather than the things that move, combine, and are connected. This primitive, naive, but intrinsically correct conception of the world is that of ancient Greek philosophy, and was first clearly formulated by Heraclitus; everything is and is not, for everything is fluid, is constantly changing, constantly coming into being and passing away.[1]

The Greek (and Zen) conceptions Engels admires, while essentially correct, encompass too much and pinpoint too little to be analytically useful. At a point in time, a society is certainly a single network, as these viewpoints emphasize, but in order to understand any society we must conceptually divide it into finer "parts" we have called the human center, institutional boundary, and four spheres of social activity. Not surprisingly, the same need arises when we view any society's historical development. While we should begin by recognizing the integrity of the historical process, we must also define more focused concepts. To begin this process we adopt a familiar distinction between two different types of social change, each of which we need to theorize.

Reproduction versus Transformation:
Social Stability versus Social Change

People constantly "make" their own history, including themselves and their social institutions. We act, form expectations, and find those expectations fulfilled or disappointed. Beginning with the obvious, we can usefully conceptually divide people's "history-creating activities" into two types. The first type generates human and institutional characteristics fundamentally similar to those of preceding periods. Even when it changes second-order features, this type of activity also *re*-creates defining characteristics and patterns of the past. We call this type of change *reproduction* because even as it alters some attributes, it reproduces core human and institutional structures. The "structural continuity" of society's defining features results not from dormancy but from human activity. Technology develops in ways such that the social relations of production reproduce. Fashions and modes of child rearing alter in ways such that defining kinship relations remain.

The other possibility for social change is that our activity creates human and/or institutional characteristics fundamentally different from the characteristics of preceding time periods. Instead of re-creating main defining structures while changing only peripheral characteristics, this type of *transformation* alters defining structures and creates new core characteristics fundamentally different from those of the past. Political relations move from authoritarian to formally democratic. Defining community structures are replaced.

It follows that both "social reproduction" and "social transformation" result from human activity. In either case—reproduction or transformation—outcomes must be explained and not taken for granted since even social stability is produced by a particular kind of social motion. But, having understood this much, we encounter more subtle gradations of understanding where conceptual differences start to distinguish historical analysts: how much change makes any characteristic "fundamentally different" versus "fundamentally similar"? And how much of the human center and/or institutional boundary must change "fundamentally" before we conclude that we have experienced a "social revolution"?

Besides observing that these questions, like all others related to concept-defining, can only be mediated by practical considerations, we agree with adherents of every other social theory we know of that it is useful to categorize many kinds of changes as consistent with overall social stability.

Things have certainly in some sense changed when a woman is selected as a candidate for vice president by the Republican or Democratic parties; when a progressive Black presidential candidate wins a substantial share of the primary vote; when a wave of mergers increases monopolization of the economy; when the steel industry declines; when a right wing Republican defeats a liberal Democrat for the presidency; when abortion is legalized; when Rock 'n Roll arrives on the scene; when a voters' registration drive adds millions of low-income voters to the rolls; when a mass campaign of civil disobedience forces a shift in U.S. policy toward South Africa. Things have certainly changed, indeed, but only within the confines of overall social stability. Such changes may occur in both center and boundary, but society's defining contours remain in place.

Changes that involve qualitative transformation occur less frequently than system-preserving changes, but have more importance from the perspective of social activists: a change in the kinship sphere replacing one form of patriarchy with another or eliminating patriarchy altogether; a change in the community sphere drastically altering relations between the races, such as the abolition of slavery or the dismantling of apartheid; a change in the economic sphere in which the coordinator or working class replaces capitalists as the ruling class; a change in political relations in which representative democracy replaces monarchy or participatory democracy replaces one-party bureaucracy.

What distinguishes these and other fundamental changes is that characteristics of both the human center and institutional boundary change sufficiently so that the way that activity is carried out *in at least one sphere* fundamentally alters. The social organization for carrying out the activity is changed and the definitions of social groups and/or social relations between groups that carry out that activity are transformed. The change is experienced as a change in society's core characteristics and thus in the "meaning and quality of life"—for better or worse.

But, in addition to distinguishing between fundamental social change and social stability, we must also decide how much social change must occur before we say there has been a "social revolution." For traditional marxists, only a fundamental transformation in the economic sphere constitutes a social revolution. A change in ruling class and in the "mode of production" is a social revolution, whereas equally drastic changes in state, cultural, or kinship relations are not. For these marxists, drastic changes in the "superstructure" may contribute to a social revolution, to be sure, but only if they culminate in a change of the mode of production itself. And while feminists, anarchists, and nationalists are slightly less insistent on making analogous claims, in practice they too tend to view "social revolution" as a semantic term to be applied only when there is a fundamental social change in their favored sphere. Of course, the assumption behind the claim of each of these schools is that the dynamics of their favored sphere are at the root of all society's most important characteristics and tendencies. Therefore, unless these change, things pretty much "stay the same."

While recognizing that definitions themselves can be neither "wrong" nor "right," only more or less applicable and useful, we remain critical of these conceptual choices because they promote all the errors we warned of in our earlier discussions of monism. Instead of defining "social revolution" as a fundamental social change in only *one* particular sphere of social life, we think it is more useful to define the term to refer to fundamental change in *any* of the four defining spheres of social life. We must then investigate the prospects for changes in each sphere in any society and whether spheres are likely to change alone, in tandem, or only collectively as a whole.

Marx himself gave us the most succinct formulation of the more monist "historical materialist" view:

> At a certain stage of their development the material forces of production in a society come into conflict with the existing relations of production, or what is but a legal expression for the same thing, with the property relations within which they have been at work before. From forms of development of the forces of production those relations turn into their fetters. Thus begins an epoch of social revolution. With the change of the economic foundations, the entire immense superstructure is more or less rapidly transformed.[2]

The problem with this "historical materialist" definition of social revolution is not that the economy is less influential than Marx thought, but that there are (at least) four influential spheres—not one—which define and texture society, and one another. The quotation would be just as compelling if we substituted any of the other three spheres of social activity for the economy while changing the appropriate references. Recognizing this, we can further see that during periods of social stability the four spheres can change at different paces and be more or less in or out of "sync" in their motion (though they will all move only within limits set by society's core characteristics). Insofar as spheres accommodate or co-define, reproductive changes in any one can easily percolate into others. A changing pattern of inter-community relations may affect norms within factories or alter political alignments. A change in industrial structure may provoke changes in school curricula and the family, or vice versa. But as long as none of the core characteristics of a particular society change—as long as there is no fundamental social change in any of the spheres of its social life—it has only on-going social stability.

On the other hand, the kind of revolutionary transformation described by Marx above can evolve for any of the four spheres from either what marxists call "internal contradictions" within *any* one of the four spheres *or* from disruptive dynamics between them. The economy can rupture due to its own motions and internally developing contradictions *or* due to changes in another sphere which disrupt its functioning and cause its classes to intensify their struggles. And vice versa. Likewise, to the extent that spheres accommodate and co-define, fundamental changes in one can provoke fundamental changes in others. A revolution in political forms can (but won't necessarily) engender a subsequent revolution in culture, or vice versa.

The point is that historical materialism and all other monist orientations must be replaced by a view of historical change that: 1) sees (at least) four essential spheres of social life instead of one; 2) sees fundamental change in each sphere as equally deserving of being considered "revolutionary"; 3) sees "accommodation" and "co-definition" as two way streets between all spheres (sub-spheres) of society so that to the extent that inter-relations between spheres are strong, both non-fundamental and fundamental changes will "percolate" from one to others.

Achieving this much yields a theoretical framework able to help us organize our thoughts about history in ways that provide us with explanations of contemporary and past events and hypotheses about future possibilities. But, if one believes the inter-connections between spheres in societies are often very strong, it is tempting to generalize further. Thus, *if* a society's spheres are strongly co-defining, a revolutionary change in one will generally have to produce revolutionary transformations in all others or, eventually, experience a kind of counter-revolution itself as the co-reproductive forces from other spheres re-establish old core characteristics in the sphere that had changed. Given this sort of interaction, which may or may not operate in any particular society in any chosen epoch, for a revolution to be successful in any one sphere, it would have to be accompanied by, or somehow unleash, a still more cataclysmic change throughout all of society—a change fundamentally altering all spheres and all core characteristics, not only one. Or, a more optimistic way of saying the same thing would be to note that *if* in some society the co-reproducing interconnections between spheres were strong enough, revolutionary change in any one of them *might* generate strong pressure for compatible revolutionary transformations in others.

Sometimes old largely unchanging kinship forms can come into conformity with a newly revolutionized economy through only modest alterations. Other times economic revolution may spur a subsequent revolution in kinship relations as well. But, what if new economic forms are incompatible with old but intractable kinship forms? Then, if social stability is to be re-established and if kinship forms won't alter to conform with the newly altered economic forms, the economic forms will have to alter again or even revert to their old shapes. This is one among many possibilities that marxists and all other monist theorists refuse to recognize, not only for economics and kinship but for all spheres in all directions.

Since such relationships vary from society to society, in tune with social conditions in each, we can't sensibly generalize about the likely strength of such mutual interconnections nor about the likelihood that old spheres interconnected to the one that undergoes a revolutionary change will always drag it back or, *vice versa*, that a transformed sphere will always drag old ones forward. What happens will vary from situation to situation.

Other Approaches and their Weaknesses

There are many paths other than our's that go beyond historical materialism and while these approaches are often motivated by desires to overcome many of the same monist weaknesses we have discussed, this does not immunize them against new mistakes or the familiar problem of "throwing out the baby along with the bath water." Here, before further elaborating our own conceptual alternative, by way of motivation we mention a few examples of flawed attempts to go beyond the failures of historical materialism.

One response to the economism of historical materialism has been to deny the existence of critical contradictions in modern capitalist economies. Such approaches might argue that post Keynesian economic reforms such as fiscal and monetary policy, incomes policies, profit sharing, labor participation at some levels of corporate decision-making, and indicative planning or "industrial policy" can smooth out capitalism's main problems. The implication is that if these methods could be "scientifically" applied by knowledgeable technocrats, insulated from politicians subject to partisan pressures, they would render the economic "contradictions" of capitalism obsolete. While there is much to be learned from these arguments, (particularly by marxists who continue to pursue the chimera of the falling rate of profit or inevitable crisis of under consumption), the struggle over control of the work process and distribution of its fruits will continue at least as long as capitalism does. Claiming to master the economic sphere of modern capitalism—heralding "an end to ideology"—or minimizing the economy's importance by adopting a non-economic form of monism such as radical feminism are both mistaken correctives to historical materialism. It does no good to "transcend" marxist analyses by denying the importance of economics instead of recognizing the importance of other spheres as well; or by denying the importance of classes instead of recognizing the existence of other agents of history as well; or by denying the progressive role of workers instead of seeing that their role is complex.

Another attempt to transcend marxism is represented by Andre Gorz, who holds that the economic sphere is centrally important, but argues that the industrial working class can no longer act as a progressive agent of history. If the future requires so much techno-logical innovation and social restructuring that industrial jobs and the relative status of industrial workers must be undermined by any desirable form of progress, then along with Gorz one might reason that industrial workers will be initially inclined to protest such transforma-tions, not propel them. And though there is certainly considerable insight in this analysis, regrettably Gorz accompanies it with a thesis that the workplace itself must always be marred by a lack of self-management. Gorz can only see the dawn of a new day in society's other spheres of life, not at work. But this is tantamount to unnecessarily tying one's hands before undertaking battle. An alienated economy means an alienated society.

Still another possibility, propounded by many social democrats, for example, is what we might call neo-populism. Advocates rightly criticize marxists and other monists for being too narrow and intellectually elitist in imposing a single focus on all analyses. But, neo-populism's critique of marxism does not extend to marxism's failure to identify the existence of conceptual workers who can seek to become a ruling class by monopolizing knowledge and skills, and, indeed, this is because neo-populism actually serves coordinator interests.

In order to remain invisible while coopting traditional workers and other social agents to programs elevating coordinators, coordinator intellectuals must elaborate conceptual frameworks which *literally deny the importance of class differentiations of any kind* by highlighting the idea of a populist community of anti-capitalist actors. Since the aim is to have a coordinator economy with workers confined to manual roles, on the one hand, or unemployed on the other, there will be considerable attention given to enlarging welfare rights to avoid great poverty and attract allies. But worker power over the economy won't be on the agenda. And, at the same time, parallel attitudes regarding racism, democracy, and sexism will also be watered down versions of genuinely liberatory views. For example, we can anticipate that progressives identified with the coordinator class will extol the importance of democracy, but ignore or down play the development of genuinely participatory alternatives to unaccountable electoral models that elites can control and benefit from; decry sexism, but see the need for childcare or "maternity" leave primarily as relating to women; decry racism, but construct their economic alternatives in settings dominated by white men. Of course advocates of this approach will claim they are seeking change to enhance the interests of *all* of society's poorest and most oppressed peoples—as reformers generally do—and, indeed, if enacted, many of their programs will have some of this sort of impact. But first and foremost, this orientation will foster economic advance for coordinators.

Those of us engaged in social theory building should take a cue from other scientists who regularly replace outmoded theories with superior alternatives. Any new theory must explain the successes of its predecessors. We cannot sensibly deny the importance of the economic, kinship, community, or political sphere and drop any of these from our conceptual framework, or deny the importance of oppression based on race, class, gender, or authoritarianism and drop any of those issues from our political programs. Theories should not extrapolate from a particular situation to all situations without being sure the leap is warranted. Social theorists who see that under *certain circumstances* pressures on industrial workers, for example, tend to inhibit the likelihood of their grasping progressive options should not then jump to the conclusion that henceforth industrial workers will play a secondary role in social change. The fact that some set of circumstances makes a particular social group unlikely to take progressive action today, doesn't mean that group will not play a progressive role in other circumstances tomorrow and in no way justifies a leap to the claim that the group is no longer an important historical agent. What more does our own conceptual choice, complementary holism, say about these matters?

Complementary Holism and Different Possibilities of Historical Change

We know that history is a single flowing pattern of interconnected changes, yet to think about it in manageable chunks, we need to abstract component parts. Many of the stabilizing and destabilizing forces of history operate on a constant and more or less unconscious basis. The dynamic that induces individuals to choose to behave and develop in ways sanctioned by existing social roles, in order to benefit from the fruits of social discourse, operates constantly, though this is seldom focused on by those under its influence. Similarly, the disruptive forces of strong human needs that cannot be adequately met by people consigned to oppressed roles in domination relationships foment daily acts of individual rebelliousness, the causes of which are frequently lost sight of by the perpetrators of oppression. Some of the stabilizing and destabilizing forces, on the other hand, emerge from the conscious behavior of social groups organized as agents of history and working for the maintenance of existing social relations or for their transformation. In assessing the possibilities of historical change in any society, complementary holism looks for all these factors and tries to assess their relative strengths.

In our conception, a society will tend to remain stable whenever a rough conformity exists between center and boundary and between the four defining social spheres. The state produces personality traits that help reproduce core economic relations, and vice versa. The economy runs with only minor contradiction and accommodates hierarchies born of kinship and community relations. Community reproduces itself and class hierarchies, and so on. Under these conditions changes will occur along a stable trajectory. Within limits, people will expect and be capable of what social institutions require of them. Each defining sphere's field of force will be in rough conformity with the character of consciousness and institutions in all others and all changes will be constrained to preserve these harmonious relations between spheres. Under these conditions the dissipative systems within society and the dissipative system that is society itself will certainly undergo continual alterations, but their main contours will reproduce without major change. Revolution, on the other hand, becomes possible when destabilizing forces within or between spheres cannot be resolved without altering at least one of society's core characteristics. Kinship generates adults ill-suited to economic roles. The economy's contradictions cause people to challenge not only work but also political forms. Community conflicts spread as cultural relations demand and provide people with personalities contrary to what other spheres require in order to stably reproduce. Basic institutions are changed. Core characteristics alter.

In sum, society has four spheres that share time and space with each other and minimally accommodate with or co-define one another when society is not in a state of crisis. Of course, sometimes crises do occur and also initiate revolutionary transformations. Yet, our point is that in the absence of revolutionary change, the failure to minimally accommodate for an extended period implies that a society would remain in a state of crisis for that whole period. We make no claim that crises can't happen, nor that they must always end quickly or always provoke revolutions which lead inexorably to new periods of stability. Revolutionary struggles, conscious and unconscious, can last decades and, moreover, sometimes societies can enter a period of great upheaval which doesn't induce a revolutionary period at all, only a period of great disturbance and contradiction. Regrettably, in this as in other matters, history offers no answers to the question, "what's inevitable?" though it does allow some interesting answers to the more tractable questions of "what's possible?" and even "what's likely?"

Co-Reproduction

In the last chapter, when we were analyzing societies as interconnected social networks, we introduced the concept of "co-definition." Now we introduce the parallel idea of "co-reproduction" to help understand one possible kind of causal force at work in historical development. Spheres co-reproduce when the dynamics of one reproduce the defining relations of others. For example, in a racist society, economic relations co-reproduce community relations if daily economic activity reproduces racist relations just as it reproduces class relations. Of course co-reproduction is but one theoretical possibility concerning the relationship between social spheres and only empirical investigation—and activist practice—can reveal whether or not this relation pertains in any particular place and time. But we should also note that since spheres must all occupy the same social space and since human consciousness tends to repel cognitive dissonance, co-reproduction is a likely possibility.

It follows that trying to overcome racism without addressing the economic sphere, in a society in which economic relations co-reproduce community relations, would be an incomplete and probably fruitless strategy. Likewise, trying to overcome authoritarianism without addressing sexism in a society where gender relations co-reproduce political relations would be similarly short-sighted. In either case—and these are but two examples—co-reproductive influences would make it practically impossible to transform one sphere without simultaneous compatible changes in the other.

Thus strong co-reproduction makes a shambles of the idea that movements can overcome racism while down-playing sexism; overcome classism while fostering authoritarianism; and so on. Co-reproductive connections of oppressions are "deadly" indeed.

Working Hypothesis about the United States

One way to think about these intricate patterns is to realize that rates of change within and between spheres may differ. As events transpire spheres may get out of sync with one another. Interactive forces among the spheres then tend to pull them back toward stable conformity, usually by evolutionary transformations of each. Different spheres never stop moving in and out of synchronization nor do they ever attain a perfectly harmonious conflict-free form. Just as Prigogine's dissipative systems move on an evolutionary trajectory as a result of complex flows of energy, materials, and information, so spheres in a society continually alter in a reproductive way due to internal contradictions and contradictions with other spheres in both the center and boundary.

Societies are always changing. During periods of social stability, fluctuations "level out." In revolutionary periods, however, certain fluctuations (which may have their basis in many different aspects of social life) are magnified until the whole character of a society leaps from one stable path to another. There is no single cell of society from which all change emanates. Instead, each cell interacts with and exists as part of all the others. To say this is not to embrace ignorance but to recognize how complex history is and how multifaceted our conceptualization must be.

In our theoretical framework, a society could undergo a number of different types of revolution. Hypothetically (if co-reproduction were weak), a society could have an economic revolution with no other fundamental changes; or a kinship revolution with no other fundamental changes; or a kinship and political revolution with the economy and community largely unaltered; or maybe a community and economic revolution with kinship and politics largely unchanged. And so on. Moreover, there could be different types of revolution within each sphere. A revolution might lead from a capitalist economy to a coordinator economy or from a capitalist economy to a true workers' self-managed economy. Or a revolution could replace procedural democracy with a single-party, bureaucratic state, but it might also transform the polity from a procedural to a participatory democracy. In the abstract, our theory of history allows many logical possibilities.

In reality, we know, things often become less flexible. Certain theoretical possibilities may be ruled out in particular societies in which the strength of co-reproduction between spheres delimits the types of revolutionary processes that can reach a new stability. And if we seek revolutions that eliminate core forms of domination instead of reformulating them by exchanging one dominating group for another, the possibilities open to us may be highly constrained indeed.

In our own study of the United States we have come to believe that here, although many types of non-liberatory revolutionary change can conceivably occur, intricate co-reproducing relations constrain liberatory options so severely that relatively few are feasible. We believe the oppressive core characteristics of the United States—racism, sexism, classism, and authoritarianism—are now so mutually reproductive of one another that, to eliminate any one, all will have to be overcome. Institutional and consciousness relations have become so entwined that each of our society's four core characteristics *now reproduce within every sphere* instead of only within the sphere of their origin.

The American family reproduces class domination, authoritarianism, and racism—as well as sexism and heterosexism. The U.S. economy reproduces authoritarianism, sexism, and racism—as well as class division. The dynamics between races in the U.S. reproduce authoritarianism, class, and gender oppression—as well as racism. And political activity in the U.S. reproduces sexism, racism, and class domination as well as authoritarianism. Each sphere reproduces the defining forms of all four.

We can conceive of an economic revolution—creating technocratic, coordinator economic relations in the U.S.—which would change the nature of class oppression but not eliminate it and, in doing so, remain compatible with only moderately reformed relations in the community, kinship, and political spheres. And, as a matter of fact, in our opinion this is the most probable result of many variants of social-democratic (and what we have called neo-populist) efforts in the U.S., should they ever prove successful.

To take another example, if liberatory child rearing, socialization, and sexual practices began to be carried out in the kinship sphere, but community, economic, and political life continued to be organized as it is at present, there would be a profound social contradiction. Young adults would be unprepared to submit to and engage in racist, capitalist, or authoritarian forms of domination. And the sexist dynamics pervasive in other spheres in the U.S. would constantly threaten new kinship practices. In other words, there would be intense pressure for the kinship revolution to revert, or for other spheres to begin transforming. Indeed, we see this happening today, with the so-called "post-feminist" generation's reassertion of the primacy of motherhood over career, among other things.

One way to think about all this is to say, "all right, if changing one sphere requires changes in all of them, let's determine which we can change most easily, change it, and then worry about pulling along the others." This, in essence, is what monists do, choosing the economy, for example, or the state, family, or culture, and then, depending upon how mechanical they are, either asserting that the rest of the spheres of social life will automatically fall into line on their own, or that this may take some time and struggle but will nonetheless be a lot easier than if any attempt had been made to address all issues in the first place since such attempts would have been divisive and diverted energies from their most efficient allocation.

This is the "weak link" approach to social change, and in some situations it can make perfectly good sense. It does not ask which sphere's current relations are most oppressive, or which dominated groups have the most righteous moral claims, or even the greatest anger. It asks, how can we win fastest. However, if a society isn't a mesh chain in which there is one most important link which, if we pull it hard enough, will ultimately necessarily cause the whole thing to come undone, then this approach becomes suspect. Indeed, if, as we think, our society is a kind of fabric with four complex, interwoven patterns, each of which has the capacity to redesign any of the others— each of which can act as a source of incidents able to initiate major change, mold the texture of changes, and modulate the size to which changes grow or are limited in their influence—then the weak link approach becomes suicidal. If we attack "weak links" we may alter one pattern only to find that having ignored the others they have successfully undone all our work. Perhaps they will not exactly reproduce the old pattern we altered, but they will mold it to fit within the oppressive norms they still prescribe. The societal fabric will settle down to a new form with the four patterns compatibly entwined, and if three remain oppressive, the fourth will too. Our economic revolution against capitalism might not be rejuvenated to the old form of capitalism, for example, but instead channeled into a new class-stratified form we have elsewhere labeled a coordinator society. But it will not become socialist. And similarly, our feminist revolution may create new kinship forms, our community revolution may transform cultures, or our political revolution may create new governing methods, but none of these revolutions will lead to optimal liberatory results without changes in other spheres as well.

When you shine a laser through a "hologram," a three dimensional image which has been stored in the device earlier is projected. Remarkably, if you break the hologram into small pieces and shine a laser through any one of them you get the same complete image (only a bit less sharp) as when you earlier used the whole device. U.S. society behaves like a hologram in exactly those areas most critical to problems of social revolution. Each sphere—like the hologram's pieces—contains the totality of defining core characteristics and can potentially project them into any new reorganization of society in which that sphere remains largely unaltered.

The Limitations of Historical Theory

There is a tendency among activists to sometimes exaggerate what their theories can hope to accomplish so that people come to believe that they have discovered the Truth about this or that. Often sectarianism follows. In order to get a better grasp on what a historical theory can and cannot hope to achieve, and on some attributes it needs to have, considering similarities and differences with Darwin's theory of natural selection might help.

In natural selection, evolutionary change derives from the cumulative effects of chance accidents in an ecological environment which "selects" for fitness. Biological mutations within an organism's genetic structure propel anatomical changes that in turn reduce or improve the organism's capacity to give birth to new offspring of its own type. As surprising as it seems, the initiating accidents occur randomly, in no particular pattern at all. What gives species evolution *the appearance* of following a master plan is not an interrelatedness of causes among the triggering accidents, which does not exist, but the after-the-fact channeling effects of the process of natural selection within a complex environment.

In societies, we know that changes arise everywhere from countless causes. Most often, whether any particular change takes root depends on whether it conforms to its social environment. In this analogy, society as a whole provides an over arching *social niche*. Be they relatively small, like the invention of a minor new technology, or large, like the restructuring of gender relations owing to a revolution in kinship forms, to prevail changes must fit (or redesign and then fit) their surrounding social niche.

Of course, this analogy is inexact. In natural evolution true laws of motion operate which allow us to make mathematically precise statements about the frequency of mutations, the likelihood of any mutation taking hold, the time for the spread of changes throughout a species, etc. Yet, because the initiating mutations of natural evolution are purely random, despite these understood laws of motion, few before-the-fact testable predictions prove possible—only explanations after the fact. According to some schools of philosophy this character-istic relegates Darwin's theory to a sub-scientific shelf in the panoply of intellectual disciplines. Natural selection is a theory which, like com-plementary holism, is incapable of alone making testable predic-tions. Elaborated further, to create a derivative theory like population genetics, natural selection can lead us to predictions, of course, but then elaborated into a specific theory of capitalist economic forms, comple-mentary holism will also lead us to predictions. Even without refinement both approaches can explain events after the fact; make revealing claims about intellectually conceivable occurrences which are not, in fact, immediately practically conceivable; and make informative claims about the probability of certain possible future occurrences coming about. Referring to skeptics who are uncomfortable using the word "theory" when referring to social history, we would reply that we use it in roughly the same way a 19th century Darwinian would have used it when referring to natural history.

But, beyond this, the similarities in these two frameworks are minimal and it is actually the differences that can help us understand historical theory's potentials better. In social history fewer if any fixed laws of motion operate. One can't make general statements about the frequency of changes or their rates of taking root since the consciousness of human actors makes most uniformities in the way history unfolds temporary. Further, in societies the link between "social mutations" and lasting changes in the social niche are more bi-directional than the link between biological mutations and changes in the ecological niche. And, what's worse, recognizing both that social conditions can create social mutations, and that consciousness plays a role in defining social conditions, in societies it follows that the initiation of "mutations" is not totally random. Chance is one factor in the motion of social relations, but in history there is no impermeable barrier between the organism/environment complex on the one hand, and the incidence of social evolution/revolution engendering "mutations" on the other. The former can cause, mold, and even consciously contour the latter, which in turn needn't be random, therefore, but can be aimed to particular ends. We can consciously cause social "mutations," which in turn either fit or fail to fit our social environment. Indeed, this is the aim of social activists.

Ironically, with less in the way of scientific laws of motion, social history permits more than biological history in the way of predictions about possible future events. The initial context only channels biological evolution, but it can provide a predetermined goal for social changes—a goal whose influence we can perceive and at least partially understand, allowing us, therefore, to sometimes predict with some measure of confidence the likelihood of specific future outcomes coming to pass.

There is, however, an additional rough similarity between natural evolution and historical evolution which makes precise predictions nearly impossible in both. It is a characteristic also common to the weather, to the flow of waterfalls, the shape of clouds and snow-flakes, and, perhaps, even to the cosmology of our universe and the dynamics of most real phenomena. That is, in these realms *very small changes in initial circumstances can lead to very large changes in outcome* in relatively proximate futures. A difference of a half degree in temperature over New York on Thursday can mean the difference between sunshine and rain over Toronto on Friday. A fragment of a twig wedged between two rocks at the top of a waterfall can cause the molecules flowing over the falls to wind up in completely different positions with respect to one another than they would have were the twig fragment not there. The smallest variations in atmospheric conditions can lead to huge variations in the shapes of clouds and snowflakes. And, likewise, the tiniest variations in a mutation in one generation can lead to the difference between a species existing and not existing just a few generations later, and then, in the event the species has a marked affect on the social ecology, to dramatic differences in the whole of nature still a few generations further on. And, similarly, tiny changes in where, how and when individuals and institutions act can sometimes trigger huge alterations in the pace and shape of historical patterns. Such volatility renders *precise* prediction impossible in all these fields of study precisely because we cannot know the position of every twig or inclination of every actor at the outset. But that does not mean that useful predictions and analyses are ruled out.

Indeed, this "chaos factor" causes us to have to understand "prediction" in the case of weather, history, and other such phenomena in a cautious way. Moreover, we choose the word "chaos" with care. Recently physicists have begun studying this type of phenomena to discern what kinds of patterns exist in the development of "chaotic" systems, and perhaps these studies will provide further analogies and insights that can help others enlarge and refine the perspectives set forth here. In any case, since we cannot know all the fine details of historical (or atmospheric) "initial conditions" as they might exist at any moment, we cannot possibly perfectly predict all outcomes at some later moment. Moreover, since the variations that can result from small changes in "initial conditions" are great for most historical processes— history's "chaos factor"—sometimes our errors will be great despite the most intelligent analyses. What a theory can do, however, is help us chart rough potential trajectories of overall developments (whether of weather or of history) and discern their relative probabilities and, to some extent, illuminate how our own activities (seeding clouds, waging social struggles, developing new institutional forms) might affect those probabilities. The task of a theoretical framework oriented to help us understand history, then, is to assist in the limited but crucial undertaking of pinpointing as precisely as possible those kinds of dynamics and relationships that will most often be most critical to:

a) Initiating macro changes in society of a type important to our lives.

b) Channeling and texturing such changes so they persist or fade away, become localized or spread.

c) Modulating such changes so they refine outcomes only minimally, as in historical evolution, or transform them dramatically, as in historical revolution.

The point is to use theory to create visions and strategy we can implement. That we must be cautious and never presume to think that we have all the answers in no way means we cannot take informed initiative to improve our society.

A Different Set of Guiding Questions

When trying to determine whether a society is likely to undergo a revolutionary change any analyst develops a set of guiding questions. One way to appreciate the difference between theoretical perspectives is to compare the guiding questions or "research programs" they imply.

A complementary holist approach poses the following kinds of questions: What is the character of the four defining spheres of social life and how does it effect people's ability to fulfill their various potentials? What distinctive social groups are defined by the organization of social activity in each sphere and how do these groups interact? What contradictions exist within and between each sphere and how do these contradictions affect class, community, gender, and political struggles? What factors influence the power of competing groups as they pursue their interests, and how do the dynamics between spheres affect the self-consciousness of these groups? How do events and struggles tend to reproduce or undermine core characteristics? How does the undermining of core characteristics in one sphere affect society's other spheres? And finally, what reproductive and destabilizing dynamics are at work between the human center and institutional boundary?

The complementary holist agenda requires an analysis stressing the interactive effects of four fields of influence without assuming *a priori* the influence of any one of these fields, some priority ordering of their importance, or some fixed form for their interaction. However, this does not imply our concepts are amorphous since they direct us to examine dynamics within and between particular spheres in very specific ways.

Does our approach increase the probability of a more comprehensive understanding? Does it avoid subordinating the concerns of one group to those of another? Will it facilitate a fuller solidarity among those with a common interest in social change? Or does it merely add steps to historical analyses for little additional insight, confusing a muddled picture with a fuller one?

While it isn't a virtue to present a motion picture of reality with no central concepts or organizing principles to guide analysis and prediction, it is also no virtue to claim to have uncovered the essential tension while ignoring or misunderstanding other critical relations. Complementary holism can yield concrete results only when applied to particular societies, historical problems, visions, and issues of strategy. We believe our concepts of center and boundary, core characteristics, accommodation and co-reproduction, stabilizing and destabilizing dynamics, and our newly refined conceptualization of four critical spheres of social activity provide a set of conceptual tools that can help activists with a wide range of priorities tackle the difficult problem of building increasingly powerful social movements in the years ahead. It is not the only set of concepts one can usefully use to try to create social change, but we think it is one set of concepts particularly suited to the purpose. Only time will tell.

*Please Note: Readers who would now like to consider a hypothetical dialogue dealing with issues raised in chapter seven should turn to page 177.

CHAPTER EIGHT
DEVELOPING A HUMANIST VISION

Definitive evidence about the worth of our new concepts can only come from applying them to three critical questions: What features and dynamics characterize our society now? What is our vision of a more desirable future society? How do we expect to get from "here" to "there"?

Much has been written about the first question. While we hope that our holist principles will inform further analyses of contemporary conditions, we focus our attention in this and the next chapter on the latter two questions.

Naming A Desirable Vision

Having argued so strenuously that societies are rarely if ever predominately determined by the characteristics of but one sphere, it follows that we should not limit our goals by visualizing a desirable future embracing less than all four spheres. Moreover, we should not *label* our vision for all of society with a concept that historically resonates with an emphasis on only one sphere. "Socialism," "feminism," "intercommunalism," and "participatory democracy" are appropriate names for different aspects of a desirable future society, but why use an economic concept to describe *all* of society unless one is economistic? And why use a kinship concept to describe all of society unless one is "kinshipist"? People justifiably distrust labels that reduce any of their priorities to peripheral concern. Thus, we will use the familiar labels as names for desirable ways of organizing particular spheres of social activity but we will use the more encompassing term—"humanist"—to describe the overall society we envision.

Constructing A Humanist Vision

How does one elaborate a humanist vision? First, we need to decide what core characteristics we want in both the human center and institutional boundary. Second, we need to develop a vision of how social activity could be organized in each sphere so that our favored core characteristics would be generated. For example, what major governing institutions and decision-making systems could be expected to generate the core characteristics we desire? What community institutions and rules for community inter-relations would generate these desirable core characteristics? Third, we need to refine our vision of all spheres in light of an analysis of how the dynamics of each will affect the dynamics and characteristics of all the others. Here, we only outline approaches that will hopefully serve as a basis for further work by ourselves and others.

Humanist Core Characteristics

How does one justify the superiority of one set of core characteristics compared to another? Where do humanist values come from? What core characteristics embody humanist values?

We know that human potentials are sufficiently broad that a number of different reasonably stable societal alternatives to our own are feasible. Moreover, since the behavior patterns, desires, and values of citizens in any society are in large part formed by the core characteristics of the institutional structures they encounter, we know that reproductive dynamics between any society's center and boundary will promote values in their citizens that will tend to justify whatever core characteristics they daily encounter. It follows that if we ask merely whether people get what they seek in some society we will get a yes answer in many cases where the society is, nonetheless, oppressive. To have confidence in our evaluations we must ask, instead, in what society will people seek and attain the most. Unlike philosophical nihilists who reject value statements or moral judgments and wonder only whether citizens in a society support it, we have to wonder whether citizens also maximally develop and fulfill themselves.

Thus, while many different social core characteristics are *possible*, not all equally fulfill human potentials. And while all sets of core characteristics fulfill at least some aspects of human potential, not all sets equally promote all aspects or foster all forms of human development. For example, while a competitive, authoritarian system may display a degree of stability, indicating that human beings can adapt even to these conditions, this does not mean that there are no aspects of human potential that are denied by such circumstances. If needs for social solidarity and self-management cannot be fully satisfied for large numbers of people under competitive, authoritarian systems, such systems contradict these needs even if people are not loudly proclaiming them. Other systems with different core characteristics that do as well by human fulfillment and development on other counts and better on this count, are superior.

To argue for the desirability of a particular set of core characteristics it follows that we must show that they are compatible with the full expression of all important aspects of human potential and that they do not thwart meeting any justifiable human needs for some groups because of how efforts to meet the needs of other groups are organized. That is, we should determine which core characteristics allow for the fullest development of all important human potentials for all of society's citizens, and which core characteristics provide for the greatest fulfillment of all important human needs for all. As we see it, therefore, a general understanding of basic human needs and potentials combined with a more specific understanding of how these historically develop can justify those core characteristics that best promote all people's human fulfillment and development. We also believe that no other logic can generate this kind of "ethical imperative." Most simply, a humanist must ask: What characteristics must a society have for people to freely develop to their fullest potentials?

Of course, no one can fully answer this question. No one knows enough about human nature or the ways it manifests itself in social circumstances to give a comprehensive answer reaching into all sides of moral, spiritual, intellectual, and material life. The best we can do— without additional knowledge gained through the experience of actually building humanist alternatives—is to summarize the collective lessons of radical movements to date in order to elaborate a few straightforward aims so profound that they can provide at least the rough contours of a humanist vision.

We reject prejudiced notions which go against all that is known about human genetics to assert that all people are innately anti-social, or that men are misogynist, women passive, non-whites witless, some people born to lead and most to follow, etc. Needs we focus on instead are: 1) social solidarity, 2) diversity of life options and outcomes, and 3) collective self-management that allows each person to partake in decisions in proportion to the degree she or he is concerned with the outcome. We believe these aims promote human potentials, reflect lessons from radical historical experience, and include many other more specific goals that different humanists might wish to promote: peace, equity, trust, respect, material well-being, democracy, etc.

How can self-management, solidarity, and diversity become the characteristics that permeate every sphere of social life? What institutions have furthered these aims in the past and how might we alter old forms to enhance their ability to do so in the future? What entirely new institutions are needed? Our vision must inform as well as inspire.

Socialist Economy

We know economic forms are required to allow for production, consumption, and allocation, and we know that in most past societies these functions have been accomplished in ways that divided people into conflicting classes causing great inequalities and hierarchies. To define a humanist alternative we need to examine existing economic forms—markets, central planning, private and public ownership, and hierarchical divisions of labor—to see how they preclude solidarity, diversity, and collective self-management. In light of these lessons, we need to elaborate alternative economic forms better suited to organizing production, consumption, and allocation in ways consistent with humanist goals.

In earlier chapters we made many claims regarding the ways capitalist and coordinator forms elevate either capitalists or coordinators, but not workers, to ruling economic status, by compelling competition and destroying solidarity, and by centralizing decision-making instead of allowing workers and consumers to self-manage their own economic activities.

A humanist alternative requires collective self-management which organizes production to involve all workers in jobs that empower them equally in decision-making, develop their potentials freely and fully, and allocate difficult and dangerous tasks equitably. Decision-making by producers and consumers must be participatory as well as democratic.

To these ends, we will also have to overcome the division of work roles so it no longer holds that some people primarily conceive tasks others perform, while other people primarily execute tasks they do not conceive. Job descriptions need to be flexible, maximizing creative opportunities while simultaneously and equitably minimizing the monotonous, unhealthy and dangerous work everyone has to do. A primary role of automation under these circumstances must be to constantly eliminate monotonous and dangerous production tasks, though jobs people want to do could be preserved. While no one would be discouraged from specializing in any area of work (whether health care, teaching, woodworking, or whatever) the economy would be fluid enough to allow people to change jobs and develop new and varied skills. Whatever the focus of people's labors, a critical point is that they will have job complexes such that the range of tasks they do will be comparable in its combination of empowering and rote, conceptual and executionary skills to those of other workers.

Second, workplace dynamics must promote solidarity by helping workers make decisions not only in light of their own needs and capacities, but in light of those of other workers and consumers. By the same token, consumers must evolve their preferences not only according to their personal needs but also in light of implications for other consumers and for workers who produce what they consume. Allocation mechanisms must not centralize decision-making in the hands of capitalists, managers, technocrats, or a handful of central planners. Nor can allocation be carried out via a system that competitively divides economic actors, pitting each against all others. Not only private ownership of the means of production, but both markets and central planning will be ruled out as destructive of humanist goals. Some type of participatory planning will have to be developed and perfected.

Third, since unequal income distribution sustains class divisions, income will have to be allocated equitably even though individuals consume different goods and work at different job complexes according to different time schedules. The economy would provide equitable balanced job complexes for all who want work; a shorter standard work week; comparable income for all; and free comprehensive human services.

Though the task will be difficult, why aim for less than humanist institutional forms designed to allow society to effectively produce, allocate, and consume goods and services in ways fostering solidarity, diversity, and collective participatory self-management?

Feminist Kinship

Kinship institutions are necessary for people to fulfill their sexual and emotional needs and raise new generations of children. But most societies have elevated men above women and children, oppressed homosexuals, and warped human sexual and emotional potentials. In a humanist society we will have to eliminate socially-imposed gender definitions so that individuals can freely pursue their lives as they choose whatever their biological sex, sexuality, and (within reason) chronological age. But how?

In earlier discussions we attributed the maintenance of patriarchy to several causes including (but not limited to) the division of child-rearing roles along male-female, mother-father, axes. Reproductive freedom—the right to have children without fear of sterilization, economic oppression or other injustices and the right *not* to have children through unhindered access to birth control and abortion—is a fundamental precondition of equality between women and men. But more is necessary.

First, a critical characteristic of feminist kinship will be child-rearing roles that do not divide tasks by sex. There must be support for single parents, couples, and multiple parenting arrangements, including lesbian and gay parenting. Parents must have easy access to diverse child-care options including high-quality personalized day care, after-school programs, workplace day-care, flexible work hours and parental leave options. But the point is not to free parents by turning over the next generation to uncaring agencies. Instead, sustained highly personalized and rich interaction between children and adults must be enhanced while distributing the responsibilities for these interactions as equitably as possible.

Second, though there will continue to be great variations in how people organize their time and see themselves at different periods of their lives, ageism would have no place in a humanist society. Adults will certainly exert guiding influence over vulnerable children, since to be a child means, in part, to be incapable of completely governing one's life. But even while protected and taught, children will also be respected and encouraged to voice their perspectives which they will have freedom to develop with their peers and without undue interference. Likewise, seniors will be encouraged to maintain an active life, with full or partial retirement from work guided by personal considerations and abilities, not economic dictates. The interface of perspectives molded in different times as seniors, the middle aged, and children encounter each other will become one more vehicle for each to learn from the different experiences of others.

Third, a humanist vision will embrace a liberated sexuality which respects people's (often changing) choices and inclinations, whether homosexual, bisexual or heterosexual; monogamous or nonmonog-amous. Moreover, beyond respecting rights, the exercise and explora-tion of different forms of sexuality by consenting partners provides a variety of experiences that can benefit all. In a humanist society without oppressive hierarchies, sex will presumably be pursued for emotional, physical, and spiritual pleasure and development. Experimentation to these ends is not something merely to be tolerated, but to be appreciated.

In general, to offer a viable attractive vision, feminists and humanists will have to elaborate liberatory visions of primary living groups, child rearing, and sexuality. But while such a vision will have to be comprehensive enough to provide compelling images and attractive possibilities, it should also leave room for experimentation and growth as we move into a new kind of future.

Intercommunalism

We know that community forms give people a sense of who they are and where they fit in society and history. However, most community forms have also imposed the heavy prices of genocide, racism, jingoism, religious persecution, and ethnocentrism. The seemingly simplest alternative to the existence of many communities which confront one another with racial, national, religious, and ethnic hostility might be to integrate everyone into one comprehensive community group. Likewise, the simplest solution to communities having internal attributes destructive of solidarity, diversity, and collective self-management, would seemingly be to redefine the culture of this one large community to make it satisfactory. But reacting to the negative interaction of diverse historical communities by attempting to eliminate those communities and their cultures through cultural homogenization is a disastrous policy. It is not only internally inconsistent, since it heightens exactly the community antagonisms it seeks to overcome, but even if it could be implemented such a vision offers little variety and cultural self-management. In fact cultural homogenization is an Orwellian nightmare.

What then is a truly humanist alternative? First, promoting diversity requires that a humanist approach to community relations emphasize the need to respect the multiplicity of community forms by guaranteeing each sufficient material and social resources to reproduce itself indefinitely. Reversing the homogenist agenda, humanist com-munity policies will identify cultural subgroups and help them preserve and develop their own particular solutions to life's quandaries, not by imposing on them, but by ensuring their access to means of expression and the opportunity for free development.

Second, a humanist approach to community will emphasize that communities are not genetic or biological, but social and historical. Their forms will be diverse and memberships variable depending upon people's commitments, not on skin color or parentage. This is not to say that there will not be Italian, black, or Jewish communities. It merely clarifies that such communities will be cultural forms whose members belong by virtue of their beliefs and practices, not their "lineage." Of course being from Italy, or having had an Italian upbringing, or having immersed oneself in things Italian are the practices that give one an Italian culture and Italian community membership. But this is not due to genes; it is due to choice. And the same will hold for religious, ethnic, and racial community affiliation. To be black implies having been immersed in black culture. Someone whose skin is black but who has never experienced black culture is not necessarily a member of the black community. Nor will having black skin elicit a presumption about one's culture (or hostility) from non-blacks. Moreover, someone whose skin is white but who was brought up in and has adopted the cultural allegiances of the black community could be a member of that community. These recognitions will greatly facilitate the potential for mutual respect and for mutual learning among communities.

Third, at the same time that a humanist approach to community will recognize and preserve the integrity of diverse community definitions, a humanist approach will also be sensitive to the need for community definitions to be internally humane and supportive of individual and group freedoms. People will be free to enter and leave cultural communities in accord with their own best understandings and desires. Moreover, cultures could be subject to criticism (but not intervention) from without, though the right of their members to dissent and leave will be socially protected. Spirituality will likely flourish though in many new forms as a result of changes both in our approaches to religion and in the character of the society in which our communities will be embedded. But atheists will retain their right to criticize religious believers and *vice versa,* though neither atheists nor the religious will be able to deny the others' cultural rights. But if a religious community denied a member the opportunity to leave and practice atheism, or *vice versa,* there would be intervention to protect that individual's right of cultural dissent and choice.

In short, under humanist intercommunalism different cultural and spiritual institutions will be preserved and the right for them to persist will be respected. Each will alter, no doubt, owing to changing understandings of the role and character of culture that evolve from liberatory internal dynamics, as well as influences from other social spheres which help erode sexist, classist, and authoritarian definitions. At the international level, as a direct extension, intercommunalism will mean respect for self-determination and commitment to non-intervention.

Participatory Democracy

We know that the political sphere is a necessary means of providing overall social coherence and mediating social disagreements. But we also know that most governments to date have created hierarchies, imposed regimentation, repressed freedom, and inflicted harsh crimes against their citizens.

When we think about a humanist alternative we must think in terms of new institutions which not only respect democratic advances that have occurred to date, but expand upon this base to promote a still higher degree of social participation in decision-making. We must go beyond electoral forms in which participation is brief and episodic to conceive of structures in which popular oversight and participation is continuous.

Further, we have to think not only in terms of a pluralism of contesting options, but also in terms of a pluralism of chosen outcomes. Expanding democracy means recognizing that there is no single right way to conduct social life since various alternatives can all embody valid goals and whenever possible diverse options should be implemented. We will not always automatically presume a single best way to do every imaginable task, but will instead experiment with diverse options.

We will also have to pay attention to the obvious but often neglected fact that democratic decision-making forms are useless unless all citizens have access to information and means of voicing, arguing for, and organizing around their ideas and social proposals. Democratic decision-making is impossible if what people can propose is determined by a few who control access to information and ideas thereby molding even what it is possible for people to think about. We must develop rich means for information dissemination, popular debate and sharing of new ideas.

To discover how best to attain such ends, we must analyze the dynamics of information flow and debate as well as related structures of decision-making to see how existing forms of each impede (and propel) true democracy. We must then develop alternative forms which overcome traditional obstacles to greater participation while getting the decision-making job done in an effective fashion.

A humanist vision of governing forms must therefore incorporate many dimensions of institutional life if it is not to risk undermining itself by ignoring the full array of variables that affect whether people can really manifest their wills in social decision-making.

A Program For Developing A Humanist Vision

If we take all these insights simultaneously, we have a kind of research program for developing a humanist vision. First, develop detailed images of possible economic, kinship, community, and governing forms which escape the classist, sexist, racist, and authoritarian norms of the past to accomplish their essential social functions in ways that instead promote social diversity, human solidarity, and collective self-management. We have discussed some means of accomplishing this much already.

Second, refine these separate images into a whole social picture in which all the parts overlap in a consistent and mutually reinforcing fashion. The idea here is a bit more subtle. In contemporary U.S. life we know that each sphere creates a core characteristic which then helps define relations in other spheres as well. The same can occur in any future U.S. society. Spheres necessarily accommodate and can certainly co-define and co-reproduce. If men and women are treated equally by future kinship relations, for stability they must also be treated equally in the economic, political, and community spheres. And we can insure this for our vision by simply incorporating that each sphere accommodate to the conditions of equity and participation that other spheres establish. But, additionally, each sphere in our future society will contribute to producing the skills, dispositions. and personality attributes we develop. If one sphere promotes attributes that contradict another sphere's operations, or if one sphere requires people with certain inclinations though other spheres impede the expression of these inclinations, conditions will be unstable. So if we want to use our concepts to create a workable vision we must be sure that humanized economic, community, kinship, and political spheres promote dispositions, talents, inclinations, and/or preferences that mutually reinforce one another. And, to assure this, we have urged that each sphere in a humanist society should co-reproduce the core characteristics every other sphere produces: solidarity, diversity, and collective self-management. Thus, we incorporate a high level of harmony into our vision precisely by our choice to have each sphere promote the same basic values.

Third, recognize that though a vision developed in this fashion will provide a degree of clarity about what we seek to attain—an essential prerequisite to trying to develop strategy—it will nonetheless need to grow and alter as we learn more from our experiences. Our tools are powerful, but they can only give us insights when coupled with knowledge of human potentials and needs. These we must continually elaborate through our efforts at attaining change and then at working and living together in new ways.

CHAPTER NINE

DEVELOPING A HUMANIST STRATEGY

"Tactics" are ways of behaving that can be used, with slight variations, in many different situations and circumstances. "Programs" include sequences of tactical steps combined into patterns suitable for attaining more complex goals. "Strategies" are combinations of programs entwined into complete scenarios for attaining desired ends. Tactics, programs, and strategy can vary in focus, structure, breadth, and intent. How do we arrive at them starting only with theory and information about our surroundings?

Strategic Thinking

Activists seek social change *against* forces and actors working to preserve existing core characteristics. As a result, they need strategies that account not only for complex circumstances and many means of acting, but also for opponents with opposed aims. This may lead social activists to consider the general problem of "winning" via developing effective "competitive" strategies. There is both an advantage and a price for thinking about revolutionizing society in this way. We'll consider useful lessons first.

Instructive Analogies Between Social Strategizing and Competitive Games

Consider tic tac toe. Each player in turn marks an 'x' or an 'o' in any of nine boxes arrayed in a three by three square. The first to get three marks in a straight line wins. In any turn you have a variety of precisely enumerative choices; the first time you go, nine, then seven, and so on. The "initial conditions" are simple: two players, one using 'x's and the other 'o's, and an empty nine by nine array. At each move we reach a new "state" of the game marked by the presence of another 'x' or 'o' in the array. Any good player follows a strategy that includes a step by step description of everything that should be done no matter what specific "state" the game enters. Indeed, it is because every encounterable state of the game can be analyzed that the situation is simple.

Now consider chess. Each player has a set of sixteen pieces of six different types—eight of one type, the pawns; two of three types, the bishops, knights, and rooks; and a king and queen. The players take turns moving according to unchanging rules on an eight by eight array of sixty four squares. Winning can only occur by capturing the opponent's king, though draws can occur in various ways. Compared to tic tac toe, the initial conditions and rules of chess have been significantly enriched. Now sixteen pieces are placed on a much larger board and have far more complex ways of interrelating. Unlike for tic tac toe, and despite libraries of strategic volumes, no chess player is able to never lose much less always win.

In chess there are so many possible paths for the struggle to follow that it is impossible to enumerate what to do in every conceivable situation. We can describe various types of opening or endgame or special structures where the king is in certain particular positions, and we can present various patterns of moves for dealing with each—the tactics of chess. Moreover, at any time during a game we can plan to accomplish some strategic aim by stringing together a few tactical forays to hopefully attain a new state of the game more favorable to our intentions. We might try to improve our pawn position, for example, or to "open files" for our rooks, or to trade the opponent's good mobile bishop for our own hemmed in knight. But we cannot confidently preplan the whole trajectory of a game.

Over the board one is always looking for a path toward an improved position. Seeing a possibility of gain, one tries to envision a sequence of tactical maneuvers to accomplish that gain a step at a time. In turn, a sequence of gains accomplished by a few such plans will hopefully yield a position from which one can pursue a final victory.

We can make chess more complicated by imagining a multi-game match between two opponents in which the first combatant to win more games is victor. Now, many additional factors having to do not only with board positions but with pyschological dynamics of momentum, exhaustion, emotions, and the spirit of the opponent and skill of his/her advisors affect calculations. The state of the game at any time includes the current score—I have won three, my opponent two, and there have been six draws—as well as the changing moods of the players, their changing attention span, attitudes toward one another, and health. Should I work hard to salvage a difficult position to gain a draw, or should I conserve strength for the next game? Should I try for a problematic win that I may lose, or should I settle for a draw and anticipate that my opponent will grow weaker in succeeding games? Can I mix up my opening tactical choices to put my opponent off guard many games from now? In other words, in addition to the playing rules, now the complexities of an opponent's long term moods, strengths, and weaknesses bear on the match. With this enrichment, the analogy to the complexity of social strategizing becomes stronger, though far from exact.

If we now switch our attention to basketball and put ourselves in the position of a coach, the situation becomes still more complex. As for chess, any one basketball game has far too many possible trajectories to chart them all in advance. Now, however, there is the added problem that an effort to enact a certain tactic, for example slowing the pace of the game by employing a certain defensive set, might not come off. Your players might fumble their assignments—unlike a chess knight which will never fail to go where its "coach" tells it to. Now it isn't only the coach who can tire, but also the players. Nothing in the basketball game is certain because the players are now human and the playing board social.

Strategies become exceptionally complex requiring attention to changing states of the strengths and weaknesses of one's own team and each of its members, of the opponents' team and each of its members, the clock, the changing score, the score in games if it is a series, momentum, bench strength, how players should be rotated and matched up with opponents, and even how hometown and opposing fans will react and the effect their enthusiasm will have on play. There can be tactical alignments, defensive and offensive strategies, and well-planned programs for special portions of the game. Even the dynamics of transportation between cities, the treatment of player ailments, and the effect of the moods and skills of referees can be pivotal.

As a last leap, now imagine coaching a super basketball game with millions of participants, playing rules that can constantly alter, multiple goals that are themselves flexible, opponents who can become allies and *vice versa*, referees who are often members of competing teams, fans and players who can join or leave the action at will, and thousands of playing fields with complex rules for how results on each affect action on others. This approaches the complexity of trying to be strategic about attaining specific social changes in the real world.

From the exact science of tic tac toe, to the complex analytics of chess, to the immense difficulties of the human equations of "super basketball," we come to the herculean complications of historical struggle. At best, we can make probable assessments. The initial conditions themselves are more complex than the whole of any other type of game. The changing states of social struggle involve endless permutations of multiply entwined factors. The array of possible tactical choices stretches without limit so understanding even just the major effects of each possible choice on different possible states of the game is exceptionally difficult. Often even agreeing on what a victory is can be a matter of great debate. The link between theory and strategy is complex indeed.

Yet the art of creating strategies for social change will be conducted with more or less intelligence depending on whether or not one has an effective means to think about relevant particulars and their inter-relations. We can play a move at a time, ignorantly, or we can play with a plan conceived in light of the best analyses we can render. Our strategic artistry *can* be informed, and it had better be if we are to succeed.

The Pitfalls of Thinking In Terms of "Winning"

Understanding the importance of developing progam and strategy, learning to account for complex circumstances and opposing forces, and becoming facile at combining tactics into programs consistent with over-arching strategic aims are all positive lessons we can take from our "gaming" analogy. But there is a down-side of this analogy that we have to be aware of as well.

Conceptualizing strategy in terms of winning and losing—as in chess, basketball, war, etc.—tends to harmonize with macho, authoritarian, instrumentalist, and reductionist approaches common to oppressive norms in our societies. By promoting this theme we run the risk of reproducing the very psychological and behavioral traits that we are, in fact, trying to undo. The solution cannot be, as some suggest, denying that we have hostile differences with people who oppose change or minimizing the degree of conflict necessary to attain a better world. But a self-conscious approach that recognizes that *attaining* a new future involves ways of thinking and acting that won't be valued *within* the new future so attained, is salutary. It can help us guard against problems that arise from incorporating our opponent, or at least the psychology of our opponent, within ourselves.

But there is also a more positive step we can take. It is important to learn the lessons of strategy to participate equally and effectively in defining the direction of our movements. But, having become proficient strategists, we need no longer use only competitive analogies. We can, for example, begin to think in terms of "building a new future" in a complex context where sometimes there are shortages of means, where project participants don't always get along, where there are factors opposing our progress, and so on. Instead of "competition," which served to graphically reveal many skills, "creation" can become our central metaphor. The trick is to attain this more positive thematic mindset while retaining the skills of strategic thinking and the abstract methods needed to develop good strategies. In this way we can preserve the positive lessons to be had from thinking carefully about competitive strategies, while jettisoning the elements of their "personality" that contradict our broader values.

Toward A Strategy For Social Revolution

To become strategic about social change, we must envision a trajectory of change from what exists to what is desired and develop a flexible agenda of tactical and programmatic steps that seem likely to help propel history down that particular path. Furthermore, we must update our strategies regularly in light of changing states of the struggle and new lessons learned about "tactics," the "board," the "players," and the "goal." Activists must:

1. Identify potential allies and identify obstacles which will hinder progress toward humanist aims.
2. Analyze available forms of organization and tactical options in light of effects in different circumstances.
3. Continually update evaluative surveys of their own and their opponents' strengths and weaknesses.
4. Envision a sequence of general steps from the present through a variety of intermediate states to a final goal, and describe how tactics and programs can help propel desired changes at each stage.

The image of society as is and as desired comes from theory and so too does the analysis of likely effects of tactics that can be employed and organizational forms that can be used in different contexts. And, to be sure, different theories yield different bases for further strategic thought. Variables considered, tactics used, and plans unfolded depend tremendously on the type of conceptual framework brought to the problem of understanding and positing intermediate goals. The power of having even a simple broad strategy as compared to functioning step by step, guided only by immediate reactions, can't possibly be over-emphasized.

Yet nothing in this says that one's style has to be stark, joyless, and automated. The U.S. Marines needn't be our model, and can't be if we want to retain the integrity of our values and maintain sight of our goals. The mindless solidarity of thousands of hands and feet moving in unison to a drill master's chants would subvert the kind of harmony we seek. Having the discipline to create and implement strategies doesn't preclude trying to incorporate joy, sharing, solidarity, and even playing directly into the process of creating a new society. Quite the contrary, given the kinds of personalities we need to foster if we are to be able to define and enjoy these new societies, these "tactics" will have to be part of our effort. Perhaps for some, the analogy to building a complex structure in harsh circumstances, as a team, and with camaraderie and aesthetic balance, can dispel the aura of militarism that being strategic and trying to win tend to raise. Or, for others, maybe highly planned out clever teamwork, such as was exemplified in the movie *The Sting*, can provide an alternative model. But whatever one's taste, the need to be strategic and to simultaneously retain and even expand our humanity is paramount.

Humanist Strategizing

The steps for developing a specifically humanist strategic orientation are considerably more complex than those a marxist, anarchist, feminist, or nationalist employs. For the humanist must deal with four spheres, not one. And not only must a path be envisioned from contemporary to future relations in each sphere, but the methods of pursuing liberation in each must be harmonized so they reinforce one another.

On the one hand, the primary goal in struggle related to each sphere is overcoming the basic defining causes of that sphere's own centrally oppressive forms and developing alternative humanist structures in their place. In the economy we want to replace capitalist forms with socialist ones. In community relations we want to replace racism and other oppressions with intercommunalism. In addition, however, humanists focusing their work in a particular sphere must also overcome oppressive manifestations that pervert that sphere from without, including the sphere's own tendencies to reproduce the domination characteristics of other spheres and *vice versa*. We cannot have strategies regarding community that contradict strategies regarding kinship, which in turn contradict those relating to the economy or the state. We cannot aim to overcome the roots of racism in community interfaces while ignoring factors capable of reproducing racism that emanate from the economy, kinship, or state spheres. Partial struggles must combine into a comprehensive strategy to transform all society.

So, a humanist activist operating principally in the economy must assess the different kinds of economics-related consciousnesses of participants depending on their class and also community, gender, and state-related affiliations. What kinds of consciousness tend to reproduce oppressive economic relations—what kinds tend to disrupt economic norms and engender humanist alternatives? What forms of activity and modes of organization will impede the former and propel the latter? What types of demands, if won, will yield new states of the workplace, consumer, and allocation struggle conducive to winning still further victories because seekers of change will be stronger owing to better knowledge, clearer commitments, or possession of better organizational vehicles or material means with which to win further gains?

Having developed answers to these questions activists can then envision a trajectory of demands, means of struggle, and organizational forms that would lead toward, for example, worker self-management through council control over workplaces, consumer councils governing consumption choices especially for collective goods, and participatory planning for allocation. But, in addition, activists will also have to determine the likely affects of choices made within economic struggle on struggles in other spheres and mediate their choices to accord with the goal of moving forward on all fronts, not just one.

Similarly, regarding community, kinship, or the state, given the goal of intercommunalism, an end to patriarchy, or establishing participatory democracy, activists must ask what kinds of organizing will promote consciousnesses and commitments and alignments able to foster their immediate goals. For example, what kinds of organizing and what demands, if won, will strengthen community, gender, or political identification, yet simultaneously diminish the forces of racism, sexism, or authoritarianism?

The humanist activist thus has to envision a scenario of unfolding events which progressively increases the numbers of people who wish to transform society and their access to means for doing so—along all four axes at once. Concentrated efforts to win reforms—such as wage increases, improved day-care, affirmative action, shopfloor council

control over health and safety, community-based economic development, rent control, gay rights legislation, voter registration, and child-
rearing leaves for men as well as women—must be formulated to
enhance the consciousnesses of potential change agents, weaken
opponents of change and strengthen the position from which movements will confront status quo forces in the future.

Similarly, forms of organization and methods of struggle—
autonomous community movements, electoral parties and campaigns,
projects around single issues like freezing nuclear weapons or
to create battered women's shelters and abortion clinics, organize
affinity groups, or plans to use petitions, teach-ins, sit-ins, or other
forms of civil disobedience—must all be formulated and reformulated
to strengthen the means activists have to introduce forward-looking
reforms and to clarify and enhance their long-range programs, maximize liberatory consciousness, open up possibilities for those who are
not yet working for change, and negate oppressive forms tied to old
ways of being both in the movement and outside it.

Outline Of A Humanist Strategy

To outline the main contours of a humanist strategy we need to
address each of the four spheres in turn and then discuss the ways
movements and programs relevant to each can combine to form a
comprehensive strategic approach.

Community Strategy

The defining mode of domination in the community sphere in the
U.S. is racism. The defining humanist goal is intercommunalism which
includes preserving and enriching diverse communities, guaranteeing
intercommunity rights, and fostering learning between communities.

The potential creators of liberatory change regarding community
relations include everyone oppressed by racism, ethnocentrism, and the
denial of spirituality, but principally those communities who are the
direct targets of racist domination: Blacks, Latinos, Indians, Asians, etc.
Whites who transcend their cultures to develop a hatred for racism and a
love for cultural diversity will be strong supporters of intercommunalism. Whites who prefer to defend their community advantages will
be opponents.

Obstacles to creating intercommunalism include the racism and ethnocentrism of currently dominant communities, internalized feelings of inferiority and inter-community hostility of many currently dominated communities, and the pervasive biases of not only community and cultural, but also of kinship, economic, and state institutions all in favor of exacerbating community oppressions.

One facet of community strategy must be the formation of autonomous community movements organized to advance the dignity of their respective cultures and also to refine their cultures by rejecting oppressive sexist, authoritarian, and classist elements they may contain. This will involve programs to diminish and finally remove racist structures in society, to challenge and finally undo racism-reproducing attitudes in oppressor and oppressed communities, and to develop procedures to ensure the perpetuation and enrichment of diverse cultures in ways promoting humanist and not racist, sexist, classist or authoritarian values.

The "Black Power" movements of the sixties were archetypes that can teach us much, though by humanist standards they also had faults. They rightly sought to understand, respect, and elevate community cultural forms, and, at their best, to refine community cultures to overcome at least some internal oppressive weaknesses. They did little, however, to increase modes of *inter-community* discourse and learning.

In the future, at the same time as communities reform and strengthen inwardly via techniques similar to those used by predecessor Black Power movements, they must also pursue programs that will build positive relations between communities. Autonomous community movements formed to help communities develop their own cultures, visions, and programs in relative freedom from outside forces, must additionally diminish hostilities between communities instead of exacerbating them. It will not be argued that the responsibility for promoting good inter-community relations lies *only* with racist communities who usually impede such relations. For though the justice of such a view is obvious, the strategic logic is not.

Just as culture will be celebrated inwardly, it will also be respectfully urged outwards toward other communities and, in particular, from organized movements of oppressed communities toward one another and also toward the white oppressor community beyond. Communities will make overtures to learn from others and not to denigrate them. Racism will be criticized and attacked, but not communities themselves. In this, as in all things, humanist activists will want to progress toward humanist aims, not simply to be "right," or to exact a "justified retribution" that leads nowhere.

To develop a community-focused strategy we will have to develop a rich understanding of the kinds of consciousnesses that tend to reproduce racist inter-community relations in both their oppressor and oppressed forms. Then we will need to assess how different ways of expressing demands and insights, speaking, writing, organizing, and structuring our movements affect these forms of consciousness in different situations and for different constituencies. In light of this, we can assess tactics for how movements can improve the balance of forces favoring intercommunalism as compared to those favoring the maintenance of racism, ethnocentrism, religious persecution, and cultural denial.

All sorts of tactics and programs including revitalization of traditional cultural practices, demands for genuine affirmative action, enhancement and enforcement of civil rights legislation, formation of community groups and caucuses inside organizations, demands for media access, movements against police brutality, institutionalization of Black Studies and other community studies programs, demands for media access by oppressed communities, marches, teach-ins, civil disobedience, and proposals for inter-community celebrations, and meetings to share cultural traditions will be combined into agendas of change aiming to create "states of the struggle" closer to anti-racist, pro-intercommunalist possibilities.

It will not be the case, as it always has in the past, that the onus for "smooth communication" between different communities will rest solely on those who are oppressed. There will be efforts by Black, Latino, and other oppressed communities to communicate in ways that whites can better perceive but the more urgent priority will be the reverse: an effort by oppressing communities to learn enough about other cultures to be able to understand their modes of expression or at least to know when they are not understanding and how to ask for clarification without leaping to defensive conclusions.

The aim will be a steady strengthening of autonomous community movements tied to one another by steadily maturing networks of inter-community communication and respectful sharing of one another's cultures. Milestones along the way to intercommunalism may include creating specific community movements, winning community control over certain media resources, elaborating ties between different community movements, enforcing affirmative action legislation, elaborating forms of cultural interchange and celebration between and among different communities and creating a larger inter-communal "rainbow" coalition.

One additional critical point is that beyond working to insure that community sphere programs and organizational forms impede racism and promote intercommunalism, it will also be critical to ensure that minimally they do nothing to reproduce sexism, classism, and authoritarianism, and maximally that they help counter these other forms of oppression. Community movements cannot be organized around authoritarian hierarchies, in ways elevating members of dominant classes to community leadership, or in ways promoting sexist patterns of male dominance or female submission or homophobia in the movement, without sacrificing both humanist extra-community and community aims as well. But to attain these ends, activists with a community priority will also have to have a holist orientation and allegiance. We will discuss the organizational means to promote this integration of movements after addressing all four focuses themselves.

Kinship Strategy

The aim of kinship strategy is to overcome sexism in all its forms throughout society and to promote an alternative feminist vision of gender relations, sexuality, and child-rearing as a part of the encompassing project of creating a humanist society in all spheres of social life. Accomplishing these ends will certainly involve building an autonomous women's movement, gay and lesbian movements, and young people's and older people's movements. In turn, each of these will struggle against sexism, homophobia, and ageism and for an alternative feminist vision of kinship relations. Each will function in part autonomously from other social actors to escape the influence of oppressive behaviors common to men, heterosexuals, and adults and to freely discover their own identities and liberating alternatives to domination relations. Moreover, as each of these movements fights against specifically kinship-centered oppressions, each will also struggle to undermine the means by which kinship relations reproduce other forms of social domination and *vice versa*.

Strategies will include demands for reforms like the ERA, affirmative action, legislation protecting children, the elderly, and freedom of sexual preference, and reproductive rights as well as efforts to confront and overcome male sexist behavior and existing sexist structural relations in primary living groups and thoughout society. But, additionally, positive programs elaborating new conceptions of gender roles, new definitions of sexuality, and new ideas regarding how people can conduct the functions of primary living groups—nurturance, child rearing, the sharing of love and affection, and preparation for death—will also be proposed. Demands for access to media and educational institutions to criticize old forms and to project new visions will be important as will efforts to oppose the crimes of rape, battering, child-molesting, "gay-bashing," and other sexist physical abuse.

In general, movements focused primarily around overcoming patriarchy and fostering positive feminist alternatives will also have to deal with overcoming classist, racist, and authoritarian forms that exist within kinship institutions. Moreover, as kinship centered movements elaborate demands and propose strategies for moving the "state of the kinship struggle" closer to humanist ends, they will have to recognize that women, old, and young people all come from different classes and communities and that even their kinship concerns must be addressed differently.

The women's and gay liberation movements of the late sixties and seventies offer a clear image of many of the facets of behavior that will be combined in humanist/feminist movements of the future. The major change will be a growing recognition of the connections between kinship-focused work and work in other spheres, and thus a growing theoretical and organizational sensitivity to the need for kinship-focused organizing to also address issues of race, class, and authority in ways respecting the independent character of their causes in other spheres and the importance of their effects on kinship relations themselves. Unlike some gender focused movements of the past, however, humanist feminist movements certainly won't celebrate biological differences between genders or people with different sexual preferences, nor work to advance primarily white middle class women. As with the community strategic orientation discussed above, the target will be sexism, homophobia, and ageism—much of male behavior and ideology, heterosexual behavior and ideology, and parental and elders' behavior and ideology—but not all men, hetero-sexuals, parents, and adults. Again, creating a better society, not the desire to be right or to exact retribution, will be the watchward of strategic planning.

A kinship-centered strategy will involve combining a host of different kinds of programs related to strengthening the self-images of women, gay men and lesbians and countering sexism, homophobia, and ageism among men, heterosexuals, and adults. Along the way demands will be adopted, tactics employed, and means of organizing and of

organization chosen on grounds of their strengthening feminist consciousness and style, countering opponents of kinship change, and
opposing racism, classism, and authoritarianism.

Some milestones along the way toward creating liberatory kinship
relations may include, for example, the elaboration of self-conscious
humanist/feminist women's, young people's, gay, and elderly
people's movements and their unification into a grand anti-patriarchal
coalition; the parallel development of men's groups for fighting sexism
and promoting male participation in mothering; the establishment of
women's centers, rape centers, sex clinics, and sex education centers for
children; the winning of ERA-like legislation and of workplace
demands concerned with accommodating women and men with
children, and winning of comprehensive affirmative action programs.

An additional critical point is that beyond working to insure that
kinship sphere programs and organizational forms impede sexism and
promote feminism, it will also be critical to ensure that minimally they
do nothing to reproduce racism, classism, authoritarianism, and
maximally that they help counter these other forms of oppression.
Kinship movements cannot be organized around authoritarian hierarchies, in ways elevating members of dominant classes to kinship
leadership, or in ways promoting racist patterns in the movement,
without sacrificing both humanist extra-kinship and kinship aims as
well. But to attain these ends, activists with a feminist priority will have
to also have a holist orientation and allegiance. As mentioned earlier,
we'll discuss the organizational means to promote this integration after
addressing all four focuses themselves.

Economic Strategy

The contemporary U.S. economy is capitalist and the humanist
economic goal is participatory socialism. To accomplish its aims a new
workers' movement will therefore have to find ways to struggle for
collective self-management of production and consumption and for
participatory allocation that constantly furthers all other dimensions of
humanist struggle as well.

The movement would draw on the full gamut of consciousness-
raising techniques, publications, rallies, teach-ins, petitions, boycotts,
work stoppages, strikes, marches, sit-ins, and civil disobedience all used
in subtle combinations to strengthen working class solidarity and win
reforms that improve the position from which workers are able to seek
further gains in the future.

Immediate focuses of economic activist attention will certainly
include wages, rents, and prices, but also quality of goods, allocation of

resources and monies for investments, levels of employment and inflation, workplace and consumer health and safety, and self-determination of job definitions for all workers. In addition, however, class-focused movements will also have to recognize that workers come from different gender, race, and political backgrounds so that economic programs, outreach, and workplace organizational forms must take account of these differences and counter not only classism, but also racism, sexism, and authoritarianism.

To promote socialist economic attitudes, struggles to increase income will begin to be linked to efforts to demand that owners hold down prices and improve goods and services in the interest of consumers. Struggles for expanded and secure employment will be linked to struggles for a guaranteed income, democratic control of social services and investments, and conversion of plants away from military production. Workplace organizing will extend from efforts to improve work conditions and safety standards to struggles over the definition of job complexes, the quality of products, the rate and volume of production, the division of labor by class, race, sex, and age, control over pension funds and employee stock, and worker management and ownership. Networks of neighborhood councils will raise demands about local investments and tax, housing, and employment patterns, which will connect with workers' struggles and vice versa. These sorts of linkages will provide a solid basis for consumer-worker-community coalitions.

The forms workers will use to allow themselves to communicate their ideas to one another, strengthen their commitments, develop solidarity, and propose and fight for their programs will include unions—reformed by struggles to make them steadily more democratic, anti-sexist, and anti-racist—and egalitarian workplace and community councils.

One important dimension of economic strategizing will be recognizing that being anti-capitalist is not enough. A positive stance must be adopted not only for the humanist movement to attract adherents, but also for it to avoid adopting a non-socialist approach which can wrongly win workers' allegiances if careful attention isn't paid to coordinator class machinations and how they manifest themselves in economic struggles.

All sorts of middle level employees and intermediate strata and, at times, even coordinators, will be welcomed to humanist movements. But it will be critical to ensure that humanist movements and their union and council organizations have working class aims as their constant priority, even as they also oppose racism, sexism, and authoritarianism.

The elitism common to coordinator programs and technocratic visions will have to be identified and combatted just as the exploitation and alienation common to capitalist forms are. One important focus of humanist-socialist activism will be the definition of work and of divisions of labor in contemporary society and the alternative definitions we seek in the future. Humanist economic movements will have to propose and pursue these aims in ways countering the current information and skill monopolies of coordinator and middle strata workers, even as humanists also seek to attract people in these positions into opposition to capitalism and support for socialism.

And, of course, one additional critical point is that beyond working to insure that economic programs and organizational forms impede class rule and promote participatory socialism, it will also be critical to ensure that minimally they do nothing to reproduce sexism, racism, and authoritarianism, and maximally that they help counter these other forms of oppression. Economic movements cannot be organized around authoritarian hierarchies, in ways elevating members of dominant communities to economic leadership, or in ways promoting sexist patterns of male dominance or female submission or homophobia, without sacrificing both humanist extra-economic and economic aims as well. To attain these ends, activists with an economic priority will also have to have a holist orientation and allegiance. We will discuss the organizational means to promote this integration after addressing the last of our four strategic areas.

State Strategy

The defining mode of domination in the U.S. political sphere is authoritarianism. A U.S. humanist movement will seek to replace it with participatory democracy. Accomplishing this will require the careful combination of short and long term programs progressively increasing people's abilities to develop their own policy attitudes and means for participation in decision-making, as well as increasing the range of policy alternatives and promoting power sharing among diverse constituencies.

An anti-authoritarian, pro-participatory democracy movement will have its own electoral and non-electoral tactics and organizational forms emphasizing new visions and new means of developing, debating, and implementing policy alternatives, and of struggling to gain adherents.

At the same time, however, the efforts of governing-focused movements to win reforms of existing state relations and develop ever more widely shared and deeply rooted anti-authoritarian attitudes will occur in the context of parallel efforts to insure that political forms don't reproduce race, sex, or class hierarchies.

Landmarks along the way might include making the judiciary more representative; establishing universal voter registration; guaranteeing public campaign funds and free media access to all political parties; abolition of the death penalty, overhaul of sentencing procedures, and massive prison reform and alternatives to prison; divorcing military spending from the profit motive and cutting and reprogramming the military budget to serve strictly defensive, non-interventionist objectives; overhauling the currently racist and restrictive immigration law and respecting sanctuary for political refugees; strengthening Freedom of Information legislation; decentralizing political control at all levels; and establishing the principle of power sharing, whereby minority views can also be implemented where possible.

And, predictably, an additional critical point is that beyond working to insure that political sphere programs and organizational forms impede authoritarianism and promote participatory democracy, it will also be critical to ensure that minimally they do nothing to reproduce sexism, classism, and racism, and maximally that they help counter these other forms of oppression. Political movements cannot be organized around racist hierarchies, in ways elevating members of dominant classes to political leadership, or in ways promoting sexist patterns of male dominance or female submission or homophobia, without sacrificing both humanist extra-political and political aims as well. To attain these ends, activists with a state priority will have to have a holist orientation and allegiances. We'll discuss the varied organizational means to promote this integration of movements in the following section.

But first, note that in each of the four spheres the same kinds of considerations will guide us as we conceive and later refine strategies. First, we identify constituencies and seek to determine how their views support or oppose progressive change in their sphere and in society as a whole. Second, we assess our means including tactics, forms of organization, and styles of organizing. Third, we propose programs for organizing advocates of humanist transformation and improving their knowledge, skills, commitment, and numbers; and for winning reforms that will improve their abilities to act in ways leading toward radical change.

Along the way, we continually re-examine tactics like participating in elections, doing civil disobedience, or struggling to win particular workplace or household demands to see whether pursuing them will lead us to a new situation with a still better balance of forces for further advance. We thus pay special attention to how alternative courses of action may affect the strength of our institutions, the number of people supporting change, the strength of our opponents' institutions, and the social field of action on which we must all operate.

Yet, as hard as strategizing in any one sphere is, the real problem, as we have repeatedly noted, turns out to be effectively accommodating the strategies in each sphere to one another in ways propelling them all toward shared success.

Toward A Holist Humanist Movement

There are good reasons why advocates of strategic agendas who emphasize change in one particular sphere of social life rarely trust one another. History in the U.S. is laced with examples of "class analysis" meaning the analysis of the situation of white working men, "gender analysis" meaning the analysis of the situation of white middle class women with children, and so on. There have been many different struggles for social change in the U.S. and for the most part communication between progressive forces at work on these have been sparse and hostile. Many factors have helped cause this lack of solidarity, some of which are obvious and many of which can be easily extrapolated from earlier discussions and from the dialogues at the end of this book. Here we would like to discuss possible ways forward.

Movements that are primarily focused on oppressions rooted in different spheres of social life can align with one another for at least four reasons. First, one might feel that members of another movement can be won over, if only overtures are made. This is opportunist; unity in this instance has no purpose other than to siphon off activists from one movement (a community movement, for example) to another (an organized economically focused Leninist party, perhaps). Second, movements can feel that alone they cannot succeed but in coalition their strength will be sufficient to deal with first one movement's concerns, then the other's. This is tactical; it involves a borrowing of one another's troops on a fifty/fifty basis as when women's movements and black civil rights movements align first on voting rights, then on the ERA, or when disarmament activists help anti-nuclear ecologists and *vice versa*. The problem is, all to often the *vice versa* never happens and unity is transitory and shallow in any case. Third, movements can recognize that they have a common enemy so that by assisting one another's efforts their own efforts will be aided as well, as when anti-interventionists make overtures to groups fighting racism, or when those opposing chemical warfare try to ally with those opposing toxic waste dumping. This is strategic; an alignment develops on the basis of deep motivational ties and though this has many virtues the basis of alignment is usually so immediate that only the most blatant sorts of connections are accounted for. Finally, fourth, movements can align not only because they can benefit from one another's victories since they share a common enemy, but because they recognize that they themselves are essentially different facets of one still larger movement all of whose parts must relate positively to one another if the whole and any of the parts will succeed—not only in defeating a shared enemy, but in gaining interdependent aims and creating a new liberatory society. This is principled and holist.

Historically, these four types of allegiance escalate in power as one moves from the first to the fourth, though the fourth has rarely if ever been operative in social life. Yet, the fourth *autonomy-within-solidarity* type of alignment is the most important and also the reason for being of the conceptual approach proposed in this volume. Complementary holist concepts propel, justify, and inform a strategic approach of the fourth type. Monist alternatives promote alliances of types one and two and, occasionally, allow alliances of type three.

The complementary holist humanist strategist must not only develop strategies relevant to each sphere but also an understanding of how these partial strategies interrelate. We have already suggested that within each sphere there will be autonomous movements, coalitions, specific forms of organization, specific demands, diverse tactical options, complex programs, and strategic agendas. Now, we need only add that each perspective will need to be aligned with one another at a higher level.

Of course, activists with their own priority focus in each separate struggle will also involve themselves in organizations and events centered in other focuses. Feminists will not only confront primary kinship relations, but also sexism in the economy, community, and state spheres. And they will do this not only from the vantage point of their own kinship focused organizations and movements, but also because they will be members of women's caucuses in plant and neighborhood councils, for example, fighting not only for economic gains but also against sexism. And, similarly, workers primarily concerned with matters of workplace democracy will also relate to community struggles not only directly through their means of economic expression, but also since they will be members of communities and community movements themselves. Likewise, blacks organized to promote inter-communalism will fight racism not only in their cultural work, but also in the kinship sphere because they will be members of community caucuses in women's, gay, elderly peoples', and youth organizations and coalitions.

The idea will be to promote autonomy in the context of solidarity. Movements will retain their integrity and manage their own destinies regarding their priority oppressions. Yet, they will also function in the context of one another, crossing lines to battle residues of oppression within the left and also providing aid to one another whenever needed. Within each movement there will be caucuses to allow members of other movements to readily influence policy to insure strategic connections. Moreover, the fact that many activists will be members of many movements will create further linkages and lines of communication and shared lessons. Finally, movements with different priority focuses will all be part of larger encompassing forms that will respect their autonomy even as respective strategies and needs are assessed to promote the simultaneous advance of each. The encompassing holistic conceptualization of society and change will support these organizational steps and also evidence the need for people with different personal priorities to learn from one another and support one another for tactical and strategic reasons and to promote collective advance. Moreover, since we all have community, economic, political, and kinship lives—even though one or another may affect us more pressingly due to our specific situation or background—we will all begin to have an interest in each facet of struggle and especially in the ways they interconnect due to the ways spheres of social life co-reproduce.

The meshing of strategies into encompassing plans for the development of the whole left will occur at every level—in movements, organizations, campaigns, educational activities, outreach through the left media, etc. It is precisely this linking of insights and their connection within holistic perspectives that will become the highest priority of these types of interchange, even while the integrity of each perspective remains an equally first-rank concern.

This is not the place to discuss the details of organizational forms—for example, the types of blocs that will align specific movements into larger holist networks—nor for hazarding guesses about timetables of progress. The work of developing a viable strategy remains. Our immediate point is that the complementary holist framework is the only one that can produce flexible analyses capable of meeting the agendas of each autonomous movement and to developing and sustaining their unity. It is a place to start as we retain our separate identities, yet struggle to attain a new society that is liberating for all.

*Please Note: a dialogue dealing with the difficulties of developing visions and strategies due to cynicism about the possibilities of success can be found on page 186 and is recommended for reading after chapters eight and nine.

DIALOGUES

Introduction

The following dialogues are an imaginary stylized version of the kind of discussion that could occur when those who hold different political perspectives react to *Liberating Theory*. They are designed to provoke and enliven political debate. The material can be read as an extended interchange or in segments, following the related chapter, as noted. The participants include:

Coho: A complementary holist with roots in civil rights and sixties anti-war movements.

Marlen: A marxist leninist professor active in numerous campus organizations over the years.

Nat: A nationalist with roots in sixties black power movements currently involved in community organization and anti-apartheid work.

C.C.: A council communist working as a machinist and organizing around workplace democracy.

Radfem: A radical feminist who works at an abortion clinic and who is currently active in movements against violence against women and in the gay and lesbian community.

Sofie: A socialist feminist active in the sixties civil rights movement and now working as a freelance photographer and in the Rainbow Coalition.

Neopop: Once a marxist but now a populist working on a radical journal.

Ana: An anarchist who works at a radio station and is active in anti-intervention and disarmament organizing.

Plury: A union organizer active in the Latino community and an exponent of a pluralist ideology.

Cyn: A marxist theorist whose current cynicism has become debilitating.

Dialogue #1: Following Chapter One, "Methods"
"We Need A New Synthesis"

Coho: (summing up after describing the methods in Chapter One) Because they fail to account for multi-faceted defining influences, marxist categories insufficiently explain not only community, kinship, and political realities but the economy as well; feminist categories insufficiently explain not only economic, community, and political realities but also gender; nationalist categories insufficiently explain not only kinship, economic, and political realities but community as well; and anarchist categories insufficiently explain not only kinship, economic, and community categories but the state as well. We need a new synthesis.

Marlen: (speaking first, as usual) Are you through, Coho, because I have a great deal to say about your very flawed presentation. (shifting to get more comfortable). Now...

Nat: (trying to stave off an extended rehash of marxist economics) Hold it right there. I thought we agreed to have these conversations in a friendly constructive spirit.

Marlen: (trying to regain control) I am being friendly and constructive. Now while Coho states...

C.C.: (clarifying for those not familiar with Marlen's politics) His idea of constructive is to try to argue us back to the orthodox fold.

Nat: Let him try.

Radfem: (squaring off) That's why I'm sitting near the exit.

Sofie: (always hopeful) Surely he's softened since the last time we were together—1972 wasn't it?

Neopop: (the efficiency expert) Listen, I'm indispensable at my job which I'd like to get back to before 1990, so if we could speed things up. Perhaps I should act as chair?

Ana: (sensing developing hierarchies) I don't think that will be necessary, Neopop.

Plury: (conciliatory, as usual) Let's not be defensive. Everyone has something to contribute, something important to say. I am expecting to learn a great deal that will help in my organizing.

Marlen: (refocusing the debate, skillfully) I agree with Plury that you all have a great deal to learn. Now, Coho, you state that since no theory can be totally comprehensive, we must focus in on critical elements. Then you proceed to focus in without limit. You've got more categories than a tax form. My approach allows us to look at other oppressions but to concentrate on economic forces which are the only elements that can bring about major change.

Ana: (speaking over the ensuing angry comments) I am glad, and I mean this sincerely, that you recognize other oppressions besides economic ones. That wasn't the case in 1972. But I think what Coho has in mind is that we all begin to see the limits of our particular monist or pluralist theories. I certainly see the limits of yours, Marlen. You ignore the fact that in all kinds of current societies, even where Leninists rule, the economy is dominated by the state. You miss that the will to dominate and the countering will to collectivity are what make change happen. Lust for power, not lust for money.

Radfem: (about ready to move out the door) Ana, your analysis stems from reading history written by men. "Capitalist society?" "Dominant states?" My approach reflects the fact that we live in a patriarchal society that happens to have private property and a constitutional "democracy." It's money grabbing authoritarianism derives from more basic levels. Who owns property or governs is determined, not determinant. Patriarchy creates political and economic oppressions. Gender must be our organizing focus, kinship our priority lens.

Marlen: But address the question, Radfem. Coho has challenged our "monist" theories. And believe me, yours seems the most monist of all. I am extremely sensitive to sexist oppression but to say that....

Radfem: Don't even think of debating me on your qualifications around sexism. As for Coho's analysis, I'm frankly suspicious. To use an analogy...

Sofie: Not physics again.

Radfem: If you put a lot of vegetables in a stew, the one with the strongest flavor will dominate. The same is true when you combine all these perspectives. The one with the "weight of history" is going to dominate.

Nat: (spotting an ally against Marlen) And if you put all us meat, vegetables, and potatoes in the stew pot together, Radfem, the first thing you white folks will pick out is that beefy marxist economics which you will then swallow hook, line, and sinker.

Coho: (intrigued by the stew analogy) But Radfem's approach prevents us from noticing the influence of different groups of vegetables. What happens when everyone picks out the white potatoes and leaves the black-eyed peas to burn on the bottom.

Nat: I was getting to that.

Plury: (learning from everybody and eager to put it all together) I find all the vegetables in the stew delightfully edible as I find all your approaches useful depending on the circumstances. To create my own analogy, if I'm building a new society, I reach into my theoretical tool box for a hammer for hammering, a screwdriver for....

Sofie: (interrupting before the analogies get out of hand) While you're each praising or defending your own approaches, you are ignoring one of Coho's main points about monism. Marxism doesn't even fully understand it's own priority focus—the economy. Why? Because the theory itself is sex-blind, unable to understand how gender oppression affects the economy. And radical feminism doesn't fully understand the family and sexuality because it cannot incorporate economic influences on kinship arrangements. I have combined the two into a composite theory which embodies both class and gender concepts.

Nat: What about me? Am I still burning at the bottom of the pot?

Ana: (enjoying the stew approach) None of you has addressed the primary question. Who decides what goes in the stew?

C.C.: No, who makes the stew?

Marlen: Who owns the stew?

Sofie: (they are getting carried away) What sex is the stewmaker? The ingredients?

Coho: (over continuing rapid fire comments) This is precisely why I asked you here, after all these years. We have to try and get out of this endless reiteration of the predominance of our own approaches. Let me summarize the existing situation. First, Marlen, you want to hold to marxist concepts because...

Marlen: (pleased to be first) Because why throw out the most important and thorough analysis of the capitalist epoch? It's strong and useful. It locates struggle with the working class but has the potential to also understand the oppression of women and minorities—in that context, of course.

Coho: (countering) But do you really think that society and history are only about wages, employment levels, profit rates, and class struggle? (without waiting for an answer) And, Radfem, you argue that marxist concepts...

Radfem: Drive me nuts. Marxists talk only of economic differences, class oppression. They even see the family as a means of reproducing the labor force. They try to attract women into the fold by organizing economic campaigns around wages for housework as the primary feminist concern because it gets to the material root of things. What a joke. Marxists can't understand sexism's origins, tenacity, or even its economic effects.

Coho: (countering firmly) But would your concepts push you to look at other oppressions? Do they help you understand differences between women who define themselves as working class, as minorities, as anarchists? (Barreling on) And, Nat, you argue that marxism...

Nat: Ignores and subsumes race and nationality. A marxist society has no respect for cultural or religious heritage. How we define ourselves, how we celebrate, play, and pray determine the base on which social structures are built. And, while I agree with Radfem about marxism, I think, quite frankly, that sexism is just a white cultural phenomenon. Derivative and not causal.

Coho: (countering briskly) But your analysis could be applied against you. If we are defined by who we are, doesn't defining yourself primarily as black limit your potential to understand sexism or classism or authoritarianism, even as it usefully highlights racism? (barreling on) And, Ana, you argue that...

Ana: I argue that sexism, racism, and classism are just three among the many forms of authoritarian hierarchies. Their constructs don't allow them to see more than one or two forms of dominance relations. Mine encompasses all dominations.

Coho: But would you, in turn, be inclined to explore the more subtle and blatant dimensions of racism and sexism or only those analogous to political hierarchies? (continuing on) And C.C., you would like to see a theory that...

C.C.: While I understand Radfem's and Nat's concerns I don't think their oppressions are at the root of things. It is the economy and the state together that create the social constructs of sexism and racism.

Coho: (jumping in as Nat and Radfem rise from their seats) And Plury would use concepts pragmatically from the theory pie.

Plury: Yes, I would take Nat's, Radfem's, Marlen's, and Ana's analyses and use them each as needed.

Sofie: But how do you know what's needed and when? What if they interact in a way that separate usage doesn't fulfill? I have combined marxist economic analyses and feminist categories into a broader theory.

Nat: (losing patience) Once again, where do you put racism in this picture?

Sofie: The same place you put sexism, Nat. Cultures are derivative not causal.

Marlen: And we're back where we started. At an impasse.

Coho: I don't think so. I don't see why we can't collectively move forward. You each realize the weakness of each others monist approaches, but not your own. You each suspect that combinations of approaches will subsume your own. You feel solidarity with those whose concerns are being mutually ignored. Yet you each in turn downgrade one or more of the other's concerns. Given this situation, what are our choices? We can continue in this manner, holding to our approaches, working toward our separate visions with those who share our theories and strategies. We can give it all up and let others determine our future. Or, we can use my new fourfold approach that redefines each of your concepts to account for influences from all spheres and unites us all in successfully building a new, liberatory society. (smiling pleasantly) What do you think?

Nat: Christ.

Ana: Not quite, but close.

Plury: I was inspired.

Neopop: She's a little out of touch, isn't she?

Marlen: Opportunist.

Sofie: I'm willing to be persuaded. Just as long as she doesn't quote Prigogine again.

Radfem: I'm doubtful.

Nat: So am I. What makes your approach any better than ours, Coho? You are just as influenced as everyone else. Your approach is corrupted by white and western ways of thinking.

Radfem: (accusingly) Exactly. You grovel in front of scientism and capitulate to male thinking.

Plury: (apolitically) Yes. Why do activists need all this theory anyway? When it comes to day to day actions, it becomes irrelevant.

Ana: (democratically) It also often becomes synonymous with sectarianism and elitism.

Neopop: (wishing there was a chairperson) Would you have us intuit our way to social change?

Marlen: (admiringly) Well put.

Coho: (confidently) Are you serious? Do you want me throw out all theory? Or just mine? To successfully work for a liberated society, we need theory and strategy and we also need each other. Our experiences and observations may give us sensitivity to one or more aspects of life in the United States, but they are only partial observations and cannot provide us with complete pictures. Moreover, growing up in the U.S. affects us all adversely. White male professionals become blind to most kinds of oppressions. Black male professionals understand racism but haven't got a clue to sexism and classism. White male workers may understand exploitations, but be racist and sexist. White female workers may understand class but not racism. Black female professionals may understand race but not class.

(reluctant grunts from the group)

Coho: And not only that. Being black or lesbian or a worker doesn't necessarily guarantee that you won't yourself reproduce racism, sexism, or classism. While the oppressed often understand domination relations in the oppressor, they don't always understand the extent to which being oppressed has flawed our own relations. Intuition and experience are important, but so is theory, if we are to avoid debilitating mistakes.

(frowns of defensiveness from the group)

Coho: And if Radfem adopts a monist feminist theory because she understandably fears marxists will erase her concerns about women; and Nat adopts a monist nationalist theory because he justifiably fears feminism will overshadow concerns for racial oppression; and so on, then each of our approaches will be skewed in some way.

(looks of distrust among the group)

Marlen: But why not just enlarge marxism's scope?

Coho: No. Starting with purely economic—or purely kinship, community, or political—concepts will lead to seeing things too narrowly.

Marlen: But I can broaden my concepts.

Coho: Not enough. Unless you fundamentally redefine them you will continue to highlight labor divisions but ignore sex practices; calculate wages but ignore cultural identity; track unemployment but misunderstand the state.

Ana: But I can enlarge my domination concepts more naturally.

Coho: Perhaps, but if you do you will highlight only those features of racism and sexism that are analogous to political hierarchy. You will oppose power differentials between men and women, but feminists will be the ones to analyze women-centered mothering and erotophobia.

Well meaning monists claiming to generalize their concepts only encompass the economic (authority, gender, or community) aspect of other activities. Starting with economics, they look at the family as factory. Starting with gender they look at the state as a complex of extended families. And so on. Arguing for "expansionist" monism still fails to capture the unique attributes of other spheres. When it is time to take action, marxists often slight gender concerns, enlightened feminists procrastinate about racism, nationalists blur class issues. Exceptions wash out in the predominant trends. Monist theory yields myopic movements coupled by flimsy alliances.

What we need now is a new theoretical approach that is inclusive, that corrects for biases, that can be flexibly expanded, and that presents an unfragmented view of reality. To use Radfem's analogy: we need a stew where all the different flavors are both separate and distinct before they go into the stew but which, when joined together, complement and enhance the flavor of the whole.

Radfem: (sorry she ever mentioned the stew) Ok, ok. Forget the stew, will you.

Cyn: (a new voice from the corner of the room) Excuse me, but there's one thing you've overlooked, Coho.

Nat: (frowning) Who's that person?

Radfem: (shrugging) Beat's me. Friend of yours, Sofie?

Sofie: (curious) Never saw the person before.

Plury: (friendly) Let the person speak.

Marlen: Yes. I'm interested in what Coho overlooked.

Cyn: (cynically) Perhaps I'm being too negative but you've overlooked the fact that no matter what the theory and how realistic a picture of society it gives, you're dealing with a very flawed human nature. Just look at the conversation in this room. You can never be successful.

Coho: (tongue-in-cheek, interrupting a variety of annoyed responses) Well, then. In the face of such an analysis, I guess it's hardly worth continuing.

Marlen: What? I've got more to say on the subject. Let's get on with it.

Nat: Right.

Radfem: I'm all ears.

Sofie: Nothing would please me more.

Neopop: Just make it quick.

Plury: My excitement knows no bounds.

(Coho rustles through her papers as the others eye her, and Cyn, apprehensively)

Dialogue #2: Following Chapter Two, "Community"
"My History Disappears"

Coho: (summing up her arguments for the community sphere) Every human society, then, generates a sense of its particular historical heritage through complexes of cultural activity. This social interaction in turn creates distinct communities whose interrelations have included some of the most powerful dominance relations in human history. But it is wrong to think that different communities are homogeneous, or that they are not fractured along gender and class lines.

Marlen: (speaking first, as usual) Are you through, Coho? Because there are so many holes in your holistic concepts of community that it will take me some time to refute them all. Now...

Nat: (suspicions confirmed about these white folks) As I suspected, no matter what they claim, in the opportunism of the moment, white leftists have never taken the culture of the black community seriously.

Marlen: (reasonable) And you are confirming my own theoretical suspicions, Nat. Your commitment to nationalism, or as Coho puts it, your monist concerns have made you unable to analyze objectively. Marxists are principled anti-racists, with a long history of respect for black civil rights.

Nat: (with exaggerated politeness) You're not hearing me, as usual.

Your concern is opportunist. You hang your principles on your sleeve when black people's economic concerns coincide with yours, and that's nice. You respect my economic and political rights, you oppose racism but you don't respect my culture.

Marlen: (correcting him) You're missing the point. We're talking about theoretical concepts here and my theoretical concepts can bring about the economic changes necessary for your liberation.

Nat: (controlled anger) Oh really? I've never quite understood that. Try as I can, when I look at so-called Socialist countries I find a varied history of attempts to eliminate ethnic distinctions in favor of a model socialist culture. To use the earlier "stew" analogy—let's not overlook the fact that when you put everyone in the pot together, the result is one thing—stew. Subsuming my culture, assimilating it, is actually the ultimate racism. My history disappears.

Sofie: (getting pissed) But, Nat, I, for one, am sympathetic to your concerns. I think the women's movement has made some attempts to address racism in society and in the very tenets of feminist theory. But it's difficult to feel solidarity with black movements who make no attempts to address sexism. Your earlier response that sexism is a white cultural phenomenon indicates to me that you care less about my issue than I do about yours.

Radfem: (getting equally pissed) I could point out many examples of communities whose cultures engage in grotesque sexist practices. In Africa, in India, in the Middle East. The failings of the women's movement around racism pale compared to what's been done to women in the name of culture and religion.

Ana: (eager to attack) And, let me add, little attention has been paid within the community sphere to hierarchies and grotesque forms of authoritarianism.

Nat: (on his feet) Once again you've confirmed all my suspicions. Is it really sexism and authoritarianism that angers you or fear of losing of your own "superior" white cultural heritage? Are your racial biases so ingrained that you too fear, like the biggest bigot on the block, that we will take over, marry your sons and daughters, steal your culture from you?

Neopop: (still hoping to move the discussion along) Well, there's just no point in continuing if you're going to take the attitude that all whites are racist no matter what their politics or their best intentions.

Plury: (trying to make peace) It does your concerns no good, Nat, to alienate your potential allies. A more reasoned approach would serve you better.

Nat: A more reasoned approach? (exchanging looks with Sofie and Radfem) I've heard that before.

Sofie: (sympathetically) So have I.

Radfem: (wearily) Often.

Coho: If I may?

Nat: The voice of reason.

Coho: Correct me if I'm wrong but I would bet that before we began these conversations none of you had a way of incorporating cultural concepts into your particular theories. Racism was just something you felt you were against. But as far as recognizing the importance of cultural communities, I would imagine my presentation was largely new. Marlen's response, for instance...

Marlen: (eager to clarify) I feel that introducing this concept of community obscures the priority of class and economic issues.

Coho: (countering briskly) Which means you underplay the impact of culture. (moving on) And Radfem's response is...

Radfem: (firmly) The issue is still basically gender.

Coho: (countering equally briskly) Which means that racism will not be of primary concern to you either. (turning to Sofie) And Sofie's response is..

Sofie: (thoughtfully) I must admit I've focused primarily on class and gender in my theoretical constructs but I like this new approach around community.

Ana: (interested) I like it too but mostly for the insights it gives me into cultural hierarchies which I admit had been a little weak in my own mind.

C.C.: (considering) I agree. I had always been critical of "socialist" societies for their tendency to cultural homogeneity. But I can't go along with Coho's formulations about religion and spirituality.

Nat: Well, Coho, I think that about sums it up.

Marlen: (interrupting, eager to find a lever to pry Coho loose) There are other reasons I am opposed to your community concept, Coho. I have a great deal to say on the topic of religion. You criticize me for opportunism, but your opportunism knows no bounds. If there were an Iranian fundamentalist in the room, I suppose you would call religion a liberatory force in history and we would all be required to bow to Khomeini as a wise prophet and a revolutionary leader. This is what happens when you lack a solid economic analysis and lose track of the real revolutionary force—the working class.

Coho: (amazed) Where in my entire presentation have I argued for Khomeini as a force for revolution? The man is a despot. So was Stalin. And he's yours, Marlen.

C.C.: But he's not mine. (confident on this issue) But I think I agree with Marlen on this topic of religion. I respect people's rights to believe as they choose, but you will never convince me that religion has any positive attributes. And I will continue to criticize it.

Ana: (with certainty) I agree. What could possibly be liberatory about irrational beliefs in a supreme authority or authoritarian structures that promote complete submission of the individual will, often in service of the state.

Radfem: And what about the role of religion in repressing sexuality and women?

Nat: Just as I thought. By denying any need for religions or spiritual life, you deny my entire culture and then expect me to join up...

Coho: But I don't. I believe spirituality is an important part of life. I think all community cultures must be given the freedom to persist, religions included. While I don't admire everyone's culture and I don't like the idea of shrines and some other religious artifacts, I think cultures with shrines should be defended. Of course, my right to criticize them should be preserved as well.

Nat: Sure, you support cultural diversity but also argue that those you don't like will have to change. Very progressive.

Coho: I argue for it, but I would never suggest coercing it. But I do expect that as other spheres change, community cultures will change as well. Yet, I also believe that cultures must be protected from outside interference unless they harm members who are unable to leave. Cultures that practice infanticide, for example, would provoke opposition from without. But I don't think such practices will persist in light of changed kinship forms and their effects on communities. All cultures that don't engage in barbaric denials of their members must be guaranteed the resources to ensure their reproduction even when outsiders don't like them.

Nat: I think you're glossing over real differences between us.

Coho: I personally hate religion based on renunciation, guilt, or authoritarianism. Irrational beliefs administered by Holy Books and authority figures who interpret doctrine to suit their own ends disgust me. Yet I will defend their right to exist even as I also defend my right to criticize these practices' distortions of real spirituality.

C.C.: You interpret God and religion so broadly that all the content disappears. Then you say you respect what's left. Your rhetoric can't hide the fact that you are really anti-religion.

Coho: It's true I'm not the most religious person in the world but that doesn't make me anti-religion. I seek cultural diversity not homogeneity. I would not only defend religious practices I dislike, I personally believe there is a place for awe and spirituality in a fulfilling life. What's rhetorical about including this under the label of "religion."

Nat: But you do, despite these good intentions, finally argue us all into one inevitable culture. You say that blacks and Jews and Irish are defined as such only by the existence and extent of white or anti-semitic or anti-Irish hatred. Since race is only a social construct, then in the end you must think we only need one culture.

Coho: I don't remember saying I was for assimilation. Sure I think racism is social and that races per se won't exist in a desirable future. However, the black community will exist with it's own culture but it's membership will depend on a complex of cultural habits, heritages, attitudes and beliefs, not on one's skin. People you call "oreo's" will not be members of your community.

Nat: I just can't see culture as only one among many important elements. To me, cultures are the foundation for whatever else we do with our lives. They arise from people's most basic strivings—customs, language, folkways, tradition—how we deal with questions of life and death, celebration and communication.

Coho: I've already agreed on culture's importance. But your view prevents criticism of your own community because you reduce all criticisms to white racist cultural attitudes. And, as others have mentioned you overlook authoritarianism in many black religions, and sexism and homophobia in some of your cultural practices.

Nat: I'm willing to consider limitations in my monist focus but, and here's my final point, I don't think that any of you realize there is more to overcoming racism than most whites think. Most whites have more to learn from people of color than they imagine and it is precisely because they have not grasped the complex dynamics involved in what Coho calls the community sphere and what I call nations.

What whites don't realize is that blacks just don't want to be around them because of the ways that racism invades broader white mentalities and behaviors. You can analyze and philosophize your marxist concepts 'til you're blue in the face; you can tell us that racism divides the working class; that community divisions only play into the hands of the power structure and we're still not going to sit with you in high school, college, or workplace cafeterias.

Radfem: I know what you mean. That's not much different from the way women feel in a predominantly male culture. Men's general behavior is permeated with sexist distortions and we just don't like it, even when overt sexism is absent.

Ana: I would say the same for a hierarchical community. How many of us can't stand to be around people whose behavior in general is influenced by being bosses?

Marlen: Or capitalists.

Nat: It's not that we think whites are genetically racist but they do pay a price for being an oppressor community and for rationalizing it. The issue to me is still white people. When it comes down to it, do you support black power? I suspect not.

Coho: I support black power. Do you support feminism? Will your community based movements be able to unite with movements rooted in factories?

Cyn: (stirring in the corner chair) Excuse me.

Radfem: (losing patience) Who is that person?

Sofie: (frowning) I don't know, but I'd like to find out.

Nat: (angrily) What's your problem?

Cyn: (long suffering) Human nature. That's my problem. Once again, you've each reinforced my feeling that it all comes down to personalities and human interactions. You are your own worst enemies.

Ana: (pleasant as always) The only human nature in this room that's becoming a serious problem is yours.

Coho: Shall I continue? Or is the task ahead too difficult for everyone?

Nat: You must be kidding. We were just starting to get along.

Marlen: Nothing is too difficult.

Ana. Nothing is impossible.

Plury: Everything is possible.

Coho: (rustling through her papers) That brings me then to the kinship sphere.

Radfem and Sofie: At last.

Dialogue #3: Following Chapter Three, "Kinship"
"Why Should You Object"

Coho: (summing up the kinship category) Every society has a socially determined kinship sphere which determines interactions between men and women; the nature of sexuality, childrearing, socialization, and procreation. The character of kinship spheres change over time and interact with and are influenced by economic, political, and community spheres.

Marlen: (still eager to begin, as usual) I am glad to see, Coho, that you are aware of the profound weaknesses in current feminist thinking. I've read much of their literature and while sensitive to their cause, I have always argued against the ahistorical character of feminism. Patriarchy is a constant throughout time; gender dynamics are the motor force of history. Come on. They call me economistic and sex blind but their theory makes them totally blind to class differences.

Nat: Significantly, Marlen, you left out the racist nature of feminism. Most feminist analysis in the literature I've read uses the term "woman" the way you, Marlen, use the term "working man." You're both describing the experience of "white" women and "white" working men. You don't address different circumstances for women in different communities, to use Coho's construct. You'll never convince women of color that feminists have any real interest in such analyses.

Ana: Significantly, Nat, you fail to mention that feminism has contributed much to the discussion and practice on non-hierarchical relations and processes. However, feminism has also failed, I think, to pay enough attention to the political sphere, to use Coho's concept. A great deal of feminism idolizes "female" traits and argues for a separate superior status through institutionalized matriarchies.

C.C.: Besides, I just can't see sexuality as a basic part of social theory. When parts of the women's movement start arguing for homosexuality as the norm, or for heterosexuality as the root of all evil, they leave me behind. Or the other extreme is to elevate motherhood while denigrating lesbianism. To me the nature of sexuality in a society is determined by economic and political structures.

Ana: Most authoritarian societies repress sexuality, legislate "normal sex," and legislate against homosexuality.

Sofie: (wondering why she has to listen to all this again) That does it. I hardly know where to begin. (Her eyes search the room, finding Marlen) Marlen, your concern for history would be more compelling if you bothered to notice the historical development of thinking in the current women's movement. Many women are attempting to conceptualize the different forms patriarchy has taken throughout predominantly male-written history. And what's so historical about your claims about class struggle? You don't even look at the changing composition of the working class concept you worship. Nor do you look at changes based on gender conflict or race conflict. Besides while your concern for the working class is touching, what, as Coho has indicated, "socialist" society is run by the working class? Are you really concerned with my a-historicity or with the possibility that you may be dethroned. And by women, no less.

Radfem: I find your concern for the plight of black women, Nat, just a bit hypocritical. (on her feet) And if, Nat, you think sexism is a white male construct, and if you think that white culture is so despicable, why then do you copy this sexist construct?

Sofie: And as a black woman, I participated in black power organizations and the oppression of black women in those movements belies the sincerity of your concern. Am I going too fast for you?

Radfem: And C.C. I am touched by your comments and support around sexuality and homophobia which has caused the persecution and deaths of large portions of history's gay communities.

Sofie: And Ana, while I respect the anarchist tradition, I just don't see how your exclusive focus on authoritarianism is going to help you understand gender differences. If parents are defined generally as authoritarian, what helps you look at the difference between the mother and the father?

Radfem: (not to be denied) And Coho, you focus on biological differences as if even mentioning them will result in fascism. Excuse me, but men and women are different biologically. We could debate genes and sizes of brains and other such sociobiology concerns but they only obscure the fact that women have babies. Your theory leads to a culturally imposed bisexual androgynous society. I think there is a male and a female principle which have roots in biology, and that one principle is caring and the other prone to violence. Yes, men can sublimate their maleness, but I think women have got to attain greater influence then men so that the male principle can be kept under control.

Sofie: (taken aback) Now hold on, Radfem, I accept the need to explore the concepts of mothering, fathering and so on but I cannot accept a society where "nature as nurture" is the watchword. Your concepts, applied to all of society, relegate men to a form of testosterone dominated beasthood. You never accepted men's biological arguments for women's inferiority, why repeat their mistake by flipping that record over? Your concepts still don't help explain why women were oppressed in the first place. Why should bearing children make women subordinate?

Radfem: But your dualistic combining of marxism and feminism has no room for understanding sexuality and sexual preference as crucial for female liberation. In fact, they have no place in your homophobic, materialistic approach.

Coho: (happy to expand this point) There is something in what both of you say, but, Radfem, by asserting a biological approach, you must also assert that women naturally nurture. Since in your construct, all female-defined activities have become positive, you lead women right back toward monopolizing child-rearing and other similar work. It's as if we have moved from seeking liberation to trying to redefine our oppression as liberation itself. Moreover, the biological differences argument can lead to other problems.

Radfem: Like what?

Coho: Let's apply the biological differences focus to the current heated issue of pornography. If men are responsible for all that's oppressive in society, then pornography is one of the ways in which men maintain the patriarchy—that is, through the threat and practice of violence, particularly sexual, against women and children. What course of action does this analysis require of feminists?

Radfem: Eliminate the entire pornography industry along with rape.

Coho: And all forms of sexual dominance?

Radfem: You won't get me to say that.

Coho: But you must admit that those kinds of conclusions are inherent to the biological differences argument. And I just can't go along with it. While I agree, and my theory reflects this, that in a sexist society and in a sexually repressed society, and in a homophobic society the free expression of sexuality is difficult if not impossible, but I cannot agree that pornography, which I define as literature, art, or photography of erotic or sexual acts intended to excite lustful feelings, is inherently evil. That would be like saying because the economy is a male construct and promotes sexism, we should eliminate economics.

Marlen: I'm beginning to be impressed, Coho.

Coho: It's the same thing with spirituality. Because most religions are oppressive in some way does not mean we should do away with spirituality.

Marlen: You lost me.

Coho: This is why I continue to argue vehemently against monist theories. They lead you, Radfem, to ignore the liberatory possibilities of pornography and involve you in alliances with people who are homophobic and erotophobic. And they require you to engage in authoritarian struggles around censorship.

Ana: I'm appalled.

Radfem: I can begin to see what monist thinking can lead to but I don't think you're aware of the dangers of your concepts. They lead you to sacrifice serious attention to violence against women on the altar of a liberal concern for a non-existent freedom of speech.

Coho: I don't think so. I pursue an end to violence against women without denying that women's and men's sexual needs and desires are critical to developing a liberatory society or overlooking the dangers of censorship. If that can be done, why should you object?

Radfem: Because I don't think it's possible.

Sofie: I sometimes feel that men will always hold to their own self-interests.

Cyn: (from the corner) Excuse me but...

Nat: I knew something was missing from this discussion.

Cyn: (more long-suffering than ever) I think it is safe to say that each discussion helps build my case. It's never going to be possible for you all to respect each other's concerns. You can develop the most sensitive theory, Coho. But when it comes to practice, Marlen's going to identify with economics and the working class, paying lip service to your other spheres. Radfem will do the same for gender, and so on. Endless fighting until we wear each other down or all give up or become sectarian from the resulting cynicism. I know. I've been there.

Coho: So have I. We've all been there. But you see only those who have become cynical. What about those who haven't? Besides, do you want to wallow in it forever?

Sofie: Not me.

Radfem: Do we have a choice?

Nat: Wallowing is not part of my human nature.

Ana: Nor mine.

Coho: And on that note, let's move to the economic sphere.

Marlen: (on the edge of his seat) Finally.

(The others exchange looks as Marlen watches Coho rustle through her papers)

Dialogue #4: Following Chapter Four, "Economics"
"History Shows It. Analysis Reveals and Predicts It."

Coho: (summing up her discussion of the economic sphere) So, while the economic sphere involves production, consumption, and allocation of material objects, it also affects people's personalities, skills, consciousness, and relations with one another. The marxist paradigm minimizes the importance of other spheres of social life to the point of being economistic; it fails to provide concepts for understanding the effect of various kinds of economic activity on human development and needs; it obscures the existence of an extremely important and influential coordinator class (pausing for breath)...

Marlen: (unable to contain himself) You exaggerate in the most opportunist way in your treatment of economics. Because some marxists are economistic, then all marxists must be mechanical marxists. That's like saying because some anarchists use bombs, all anarchists are mad-bombers.

Coho: Calling me opportunist doesn't address the questions I've raised. I don't deny that most marxists add qualitative concerns to their economic science, but they hamper their efforts by removing it from their most basic guiding concepts. For instance, I find nothing in your labor theory of value that takes qualities into account.

Marlen: Well, I...

Coho: In fact, your labor theory of value reduces all matters to "hours of labor." Quality of work and consumption, mindsets and social relations of workers and consumers have no impact on a) values and exchange rates; and b) quality and character of who we are and what we do.

Marlen: If you would let me get a word in...

Coho: While your concepts have resulted in rich investigation into classes, your final class definitions have little to say about workplace relations except as they relate to ownership.

Marlen: I...

Nat: And what does the labor theory of value have to say about the importance of workers' cultural heritage, community identity, and the often intense racism of the white working class?

Marlen: You know my record in working against income differentials, divisions that weaken the working class.

Coho: But your concepts prevent you from seeing that workplace relations, job definitions, chains of command, workplace culture, consumption patterns, and prices are also partially defined by non-class forces.

Marlen: (confident) Of course we recognize the importance of seeing women as economic actors. Big deal. Women are secretaries more often than men.

Sofie: (sarcastic) And capitalists are rich more often than workers. Can you explain gender divisions of labor? Or why, when men and women hold the same position, men are paid more? Or why, when men take jobs that have been considered "women's" jobs, those jobs suddenly change, not just in salary levels, but in quality and status? Your categories ensure that you don't ask those questions; that you don't even know to ask those questions.

Marlen: I think our analysis of the working class, both women and men, gives some insights into these questions and I fail to see...

Coho: Precisely my point. You do fail to see. You overlook influences that affect how people see and relate to one another, the complexity of people's different interests, and therefore how we are likely to relate to political and economic programs and events.

Ana: And you also fail to see that marxism has never in practice meant liberation for the working class. Your concepts recreate authority dynamics through a socialist state.

Nat: And you also fail to fully understand the working class because you are talking only of the white working class. Much of what you think, do and say is geared to appeal to a white working class culture.

Radfem: A white male working class culture.

Marlen: (not impressed) Your arguments expose your failure to comprehend marxism as a theory of the working class and, more importantly, a theory for revolution and liberation.

Coho: But what marxist guided revolution has been led by the working class? And what resulting society has been controlled by the working class? Marxism has given us insights into capitalism but it has failed to give us a theory of socialism. Your preferred societies are run by coordinators, not workers.

C.C.: (on firm ground here) You're criticizing Leninism, not marxism. I wouldn't call Soviet states marxist. As a marxist, I oppose all forms which subjugate workers. I agree that orthodox marxism overlooks certain factors but you fail to recognize that there are marxist strains that have done much better, council communism, for instance. While we are slow to understand the role of gender and race, we are trying to expand and change.

Coho: But since you are a relatively small offshoot, your tenets are swallowed up by the enormity of the marxist heritage you attempt to contradict.

C.C.: Complementary holism doesn't exactly have a huge following either.

Coho: If that's still true when we've existed as long as council communism has, then I will concede the point. However, that isn't my only criticism.

C.C.: I had a feeling it wasn't.

Coho: To me council communism is a merger of marxism and anarchism in the same way that socialist feminism is a merger of marxism and feminism. Like the best socialist feminists, the best council communists have altered their component theories to incorporate economic and political insights particularly around the concepts of self-management. But you fail to criticize all the failings of the theories you combine. You think the main weakness of marxism is only its Leninist strategic baggage while you overlook more basic conceptual limitations.

Marlen: (eager to reclaim the discussion) This is outrageous. You confuse lack of perfect practice with inherent theoretical failings. Because bureaucratic states have usurped power in certain countries, you want to throw out the entire marxist vision. A democratic state alongside a centrally planned economy will serve the class which ultimately administers it, the working class. After all, we are, by your own admittance, Coho, searching for theoretical constructs that give us the best chance for the broadest kind of success. From there we can move to perfect it. If we wait to find the broadest possible lowest common denominator theory we will wait until the cows come home, the stew is a crust on the bottom of the pan, the earth has disappeared into a black hole—use any analogy you want.

Coho: Why do you fail to...

Marlen: (only beginning to assert the weight of history) Let me finish. Nat, you claim concern for the black community but you fail to define and understand capitalism which oppresses all people. To assert your cultural heritage and religion at the expense of a working class revolution seems a luxury we cannot afford. In fact, many in your movement argue for black capitalism. And Radfem, your theory ignores that men are oppressed as well as oppressors. And Ana, your theory tells you nothing about capitalist encirclement. You are so worried about hierarchies you barely mention poverty, occupational health and safety, wages, pensions, and so on.

Coho: But you keep arguing my case for me. Why wouldn't you prefer theoretical concepts that allowed you to do all of what you just described? Why argue for one that largely excludes all or a combination of them? Why do you hold to a monist framework and insist on its dominance? We've all seen how your central planning works. It elevates central planners, managers, intellectual workers, not the working class.

Neopop: But someone has to administer an economy. The issue is: who do they serve?

Marlen: Quite right. In a capitalist society your coordinators are tools of the capitalists. Coordinators in a socialist society are in the service of workers.

Coho: Coordinators won't exist in a socialist society. In your vision, they rule. Sometimes workers in capitalism blindly serve capitalists, yet you have no trouble identifying them as a separate and potentially revolutionary class. Coordinators too can be conscious of their economic position and struggle for ruling status. Marxism's focus on capitalism's economic failures and celebration of central planning lays the perfect basis for coordinator control of your so-called working class revolution. Coordinators argue for their superior intellectual skills when they promote central planning, markets, or the best economic uses of technology. The Marxist program allows coordinators to offer some worthwhile benefits to win workers' allegiance in exchange for coordinator control. In Marxist Leninist societies, for example, the state bureaucracy only took on the double duty of planning the economic and political spheres because there weren't enough coordinators to do the job. So the state...

Ana: Became lord of all.

Coho: In many western societies, coordinators would be able to administer a centrally planned economy alongside a parliamentary state, which would be in their interest. Eurocommunists have dropped the notion of dictatorship of the proletariat, party, or anyone else for just that reason.

C.C.: I can't argue with that. But I would not describe the societies you refer to as socialist.

Marlen: (in disbelief) I'm in a vacuum of a-historical nonsense. You ignore capitalist encirclement and the poverty and illiteracy that has held back marxist revolutions. You ignore that marxism is read, studied, and adopted by a majority of the world's population. It has been the theoretical motor for huge historical transformations.

Coho: And I have continually given marxism its due. But we must critique the failings of its theoretical concepts in light of our desire to bring about true liberation for all spheres of society. The Russian revolution has had decades of history to play itself out. The problems in Soviet society can no longer be blamed solely on outside factors. The Soviet Union is a superpower. East Germany and Czechoslovakia, both industrialized countries when they had the Soviet model rammed down their collective throats, have the same basic failings. If the marxism that informs these models is so good, why do these problems still exist? Because marxism is a theory geared toward the interests of coordinators, that's why. History shows it, analysis reveals and predicts it. Coordinator programs and so-called working class organizations display it. (pausing to catch her breath)

Marlen: (feebly but still not convinced) But marxism has also shown that it can change over time, that it can incorporate such recognitions.

C.C.: And it is important to be identified with that tradition. We live and work in a capitalist country that obscures it's oppressive economic values with rhetoric about democracy and makes it difficult for people to see the effect of capitalism on daily life. Marxism has fueled opposition...

Coho: Yes, and it's not that all marxists won't change, it's that not enough will. What changes have you yourself made, Marlen, even when under incredible pressure from black power and women's movements. And, C.C., most marxists would rather not include you in their camp since you argue for things they don't really want...like self-management. The differences between you and other marxists are so great that using the term marxist doesn't really describe what you believe. (pausing for breath)

Marlen: I...

Coho: Marxism has been a powerful tool for understanding the injustices of capitalism. But the fact that it emphasizes capitalism's under-utilization and misdirection of productive capabilities can serve a coordinator as well as a socialist view. Coordinators feel they can reorient technology and be more productive and humane by replacing pursuit of profit with elite administration. And marxism's celebration of central planning or markets, productivity and efficiency, fits in well with coordinator aims.

Marlen: I...

Coho: Yes?

Marlen: I'm thinking.

Coho: While you're thinking, why don't we move to the political sphere?

Ana: (pleased with herself) I'm ready.

Marlen: (still thinking) I'm not.

Plury: I can see why. That was an onslaught. I was about to side with Marlen, just out of sympathy.

Nat: Not me. I feel the weight of history removed from my shoulders.

Cyn: (from the corner smugly) Excuse me but—

(the group scowls at the figure in the corner)

Coho: Yes, Cyn?

Cyn: You want history? I'll give you history. History shows there will always be bosses and those who are bossed. It's human nature.

Sofie: (muttering to Nat) Again with this human nature.

Cyn: Sure, I once believed that all this was possible. Then I tried working with people, organizing to build a movement for change. We spent the entire time fighting, arguing to win out over each other. The result? No one could work with anyone else. You can't bring about change with thousands of parties each made up of one person.

(Angry looks focus on the corner chair)

Radfem: (on the edge of her chair) Want me to remove this person, Coho? I need some exercise.

Nat: (halfway up) You want human nature, Cyn, I'll show you human nature.

Coho: I'd rather discuss with Ana the weaknesses of her theory regarding the political sphere.

Ana: (sighing as the others settle down) Be my guest.

Dialogue #5: Following Chapter Five, "Politics"
"The Theory Is Often Better Than The Practice"

Coho: (bringing her political sphere discussion to a close) And so depending on the character of the political sphere, people will be hierarchically arrayed accordingly. Whatever form the state takes, political relations influence not only the distribution of governmental decision-making power but the consciousness which people bring to the economic, kinship, and community spheres. And political relations greatly affect the ways social institutions mediate and disseminate information and misinformation.

Marlen: (a little daunted from the economy conversation but still eager to begin as usual) The absence of any economic analysis renders anarchist concepts practically useless. In addition, they are so obsessed with hierarchies that many anarchists oppose all forms of organization, including democratic states, unions, and political parties.

Sofie: (friendly but concerned) I have to agree with Marlen's criticism of your lack of economic analysis, Ana. But also, I find that anarchism does not provide a way of understanding how state structures vary according to patriarchal influences. And while most anarchists oppose hierarchical relations between men and women, adults and children, they don't understand the bases of these hierarchies as they stem from kinship relations or why these hierarchies persist.

Radfem: (friendly but also concerned) I, too, have found much to admire in the often passionate and eloquent writings and actions of anarchists against authoritarianism. But I have to admit, Ana, that while individual anarchists personally oppose homophobia and sexual repression, their opposition seems to be based more on opposition to state intervention than a real understanding of the issues involved. Or to a commitment to a non-heterosexually dominated society.

Nat: (dubious but friendly) I find your concern for minority rights and concerns even less impressive than Marlen's, Sofie's, and Radfem's. Your analysis doesn't look at the complexity of racial oppression, or how state structures vary depending on splits in community spheres.

Coho: That's certainly true. Like marxists, anarchists tend to see only the ways that community forms support the oppression they want to eliminate, not how they meet human needs.

Ana: (responding in a friendly fashion) We anarchists are often free and open to new concepts so I have no trouble, unlike some of you, admitting that I'm starting to like Coho's approach quite a bit. Particularly it's criticism of marxism.

Plury: Something's wrong here. This is all too friendly.

Ana: But...

Plury: Spoke too soon.

Ana: Let me remind each of you, in the spirit of comradeship, mind you, of a few things. First, Marlen, you don't criticize state power or workplace hierarchies. Is that because you believe in them? Have you carved a place for yourself at the top of one of them? And Sofie, while I appreciate your supportive comments and the application of anarchist tenets by the women's movement, I have also found that many women's organizations and individual feminists stop criticizing other's power once they have gained a little themselves. Nor have I seen incredible efforts by the women's movement to criticize state power. I have seen more efforts to have equal access to that power. And Radfem, your theory simply posits a new authority––that of women over men, homosexuality over heterosexuality. And Nat, while the civil rights movement was infused with the spirit if not the practice of democracy, the black power movements were the most hierarchical I've seen. Or is this a white construct? And Neopop...well, you get the idea. Each one of your spheres has not dealt adequately with questions of power.

Coho: Well put. I agree. But I think anarchists themselves could be criticized for the very same thing. I don't think that anarchists suffer only from overemphasizing political hierarchies as the cause of all others; or for failing to recognize kinship, community and economic spheres. Anarchists also fail to adequately describe the state itself. You identify intrinsic power dynamics but you don't then go on to understand the intricacies of bureaucracy or the means of information and communication control tied in with varying types of state relations. In short, your analysis is too simplified.

Ana: (friendly to the end) So the theory is often better than the practice. I am already willing to broaden my framework. But at the risk of seeming monist, Coho, how can we weave all these spheres together into one holistic cloth that avoids new forms of dominance and subsumption?

Cyn: (leaning forward in the chair in the corner) I can answer that. You can't.

Ana: (with a supreme effort at friendliness) We appreciate your constructive comments, Cyn...

Coho: (rustling papers over the hostile mutterings destroying the friendly atmosphere) Now, to continue on to society.

Dialogue #6: Following Chapter Six, "Society"
"I Do Get A Little Carried Away"

Coho: (warming to her task in a summing up of the strengths of complementary holism as a method for better understanding societies) And so holism emphasizes that all human activity affects all four spheres of human existence. Once more it asserts that any hierarchy of influence in a particular society must be empirically demonstrated. Holism recognizes the connectivity of spheres so that spheres exist always in the context of a whole that defines them all.

Marlen: (with renewed vigor) It still seems suicidal to me to throw out an already existing powerful materialist theory. Your complementary holist approach is all concepts and no theory. Why not build carefully from an economic theory that is universal?

Nat: (not giving up) Still at it, Marlen? Why not take the community sphere and build off that?

Radfem: (not giving up either) The kinship sphere.

Ana: (reminding them) The political sphere.

Coho: But it's true that we still need to apply complementary holist concepts to generate specific theories of particular societies.

Marlen: (challenging) What does your framework help you to understand about the Soviet Union, for instance, that I would ignore?

Coho: (taking up the challenge) You look at the Soviet Union and see a deformed socialist society. The economy to you has socialist forms, the state is a bureaucracy. You proceed to blame these details on poverty, capitalist encirclement, Stalinism, problems located within the state, prior history, or other countries. You analyze in detail the intricate problems of the Soviet planning system, bemoaning its centralization and subordination to the Party, but you never see the forest for the trees. The Soviet Union has neither a capitalist nor a socialist mode of production.

C.C.: (contributing) And as I understand it, Coho, your complementary holist approach, correct me if I'm wrong, would give a completely different view. You would describe a coordinator economic sphere in which planners, managers, and other conceptual workers occupy positions of ruling economic status. And you would see a bureaucratic dictatorial state which still in part administers the economy because in the early days there weren't enough coordinators to do the job—and because workers self-management was anathema to Leninists.

Nat: And, have I got this right, Coho, wouldn't your approach allow you to see a complex community sphere in the Soviet Union in which minority cultural communities struggle for dignity against forces that seek to reduce cultural variety to dominant Russian norms? Assimilation with respect, you might call it, or more aptly, cultural homogenization.

Marlen: (with certainty) You are so obsessed with maintaining your heritage, Nat, that you fail to appreciate the struggle to create a new socialist culture.

Nat: New cultural forms that trample spiritual life and whose aesthetics emphasize socialist realism; this is not a culture I would fight to create.

Sofie: And, add to this Coho if I leave something out, wouldn't your approach see a patriarchal kinship sphere in the Soviet Union in which women suffer domination at the hands of sexist men. And while institutional structures differ from those in the U.S., they are patriarchal nonetheless.

Radfem: And, if I've understood Coho correctly, the entire question of sexuality, sexual preference, subtle and not so subtle gender divisions throughout society would only be peripherally considered by a marxist analysis.

Marlen: (holding fast) I am not convinced that an expanded monist approach isn't the most useful for our purposes.

Ana: But, if I may explain what Coho's getting at here. An enlightened monism in the hands of a clever marxist simply expands a narrow economic focus. Factory work as first-cause gives way to production in general, which becomes all economic activity which gives way to a concept that emphasizes not only production and consumption but reproduction in the factory and the family, which grows to encompass production and reproduction of ideas, people, and culture.

C.C.: Even the definition of class, am I right, Coho, expands to encompass features rooted in sexual, political, and cultural divisions of labor. But it is all based on economic/material features...

Sophie: And so it too narrow. For example, when economic concepts are extended to incorporate kinship relations, they only address kinship attributes insofar as they are analogous to production and consumption...

Radfem: To see income differentials more than sexual norms of teenagers; job structures more than courtship practices and marriage vows; divisions of labor in the home rather than violence against women. No expansion of economy-based concepts will enlighten anyone about erotophobia.

Nat: What's more, even the most enlightened monist theories scare off activists. I must admit, white workers don't coalesce around black nationalist ideology and certainly black nationalists won't support class demands that appear to apply to whites only.

Plury: But you've very neatly argued for my pluralist approach—all these oppressions exist and it's simply a question of picking the right tool for the job.

Sofie: If I may, Coho? The difference between pluralism and Coho's approach is that the latter stresses the fact that we all simultaneously identify as members of classes, gender groups, communities, and political hierarchies. And this holistic experience of society determines how we each relate to our surroundings and what we expect from life.

Ana: For instance, Radfem asks questions about gender and sexuality, Marlen asks questions about forces and relations of production and class struggle, Nat asks questions about culture and spirituality, I ask about politics and hierarchies. But Coho proposes an approach that makes it easier to ask more encompassing questions and to see important relationships—not just using one sphere here, one sphere there.

Plury: I still don't see the difference. I think Coho's just obscuring the issue unnecessarily.

Coho: Take the Soviet example again. The complementary holist approach helps us look at struggles within the Soviet coordinator class over the relative importance of market and planning forms; between workers and coordinators over management prerogatives; between coordinators and political bureaucrats over cultural definitions and rights; and among genders over divisions in role structures from the earliest days of the Soviet revolution.

C.C.: Yes, I think we're all beginning to see the possibilities.

Coho: But what you're not seeing, I think, is...

Plury: I knew there'd be something.

Coho: Those involved in each particular sphere must be able to understand not only the concerns and dynamics of other spheres but the interactive effects of trends within spheres on other spheres.

Plury: This is so confusing.

Coho: (with emphasis) And to see the implications of these interactions on visions and strategies for change. To see the impossibility of building a liberatory theory, strategy and vision when separate conceptualizations and their movements are "out of sync"; when their relationship is not complementary but antagonistic.

Radfem: (wearily) You know, Coho, the more you argue with us, the more you attack Marlen, in particular, the more I begin to see the same dynamics that made me opt for movement separatism. It all begins to sound so "holier than thou."

Coho: Perhaps I do get a little carried away.

Sofie: I must admit that I cringe every time your scientific analogies become almost a basis for "proving" the correctness of your concepts.

Coho: I do get excited over my charts and spheres, but I don't mean my analogies as proofs...

C.C.: After all, Coho, what prevents the very inclusiveness and flexibility of your system from becoming as dogmatic as you describe ours to be—particularly Marlen's?

Coho: I was just trying to...

Plury: And, as I said earlier, what keeps your system from being so abstract, so intellectual that only you and a few others can constructively apply it?

Neopop: On the contrary, I think the weakness of Coho's system is that she says too little about who would administer it. Who would take leadership?

Nat: It's true that while I find myself developing a real affinity for Coho's approach and it's potential I still can't picture myself involved in organizing for voter registration by talking about "social moments."

Ana: There seems to be something wrong with creating a tight intellectual system and calling it a theory of society or history. It still requires the arguing for and imposition of one system over another. Our interpersonal dynamics are centered around one person trouncing another, bludgeoning another.

Radfem: Instead of being more marxist than thou, more feminist than thou, more theoretical than thou...

Marlen: (smiling) We can be more cohoist than thou.

Coho: Are you arguing that there is no difference between a system which argues for the exclusion of others, as each of yours does, and a system which argues for the inclusion of others, as complementary holism does? Between a system which argues for the elitist power of its adherents and a system that argues against elitism? Certainly there is something grandiose about trying to enunciate a theory of history when we know so little. It's time to organize around a theory that recognizes it's limitations, that attempts to generate a democratic movement around shared ways of thinking about the world and a better future.

Plury: Sounds like a step forward from sectarian isolation, organizing around stars and leaders, with temporary slogans and fears, and with no shared coherent intellectual framework.

Coho: Exactly. Regardless of the dangers, we have to embrace a theory and vision. We'd better make sure that the concepts we choose are as useful, creative, and anti-sectarian as possible.

(a pause, then a familiar voice from the corner)

Cyn: (softly, wearily) No one wants that more than I. Historically it's never been done.

Coho: (over the ensuing groans) Since you mention it, Cyn, let's take a look at what history shows.

(gloom begins to settle as they eye Coho happily rustling through her papers)

Dialogue #7: Following Chapter Seven, "History"
"Like I Said; No Laws Of Motion"

Coho: (finishing her summary discussion of history and social change) And so, the point is that historical materialism and all other monist orientations must be replaced by a view of historical change that: sees at least four essential spheres of social life instead of one; sees fundamental change in each sphere as equally deserving of being considered revolutionary; and sees accommodation and codefinition as two way streets between spheres so that fundamental and non-fundamental changes will percolate from one to others.

Marlen: (this is his turf and he is first, as usual) I think you have really lost it this time, Coho. You cannot point to any inexorable processes regarding kinship, authority, and community that lead inevitably to revolutionary contradictions. Why don't you finally admit that economics directs historical developments? Accumulation causes contradictions rupturing old forms and auguring new ones. Other social dynamics, as I have stated, are important primarily in terms of their effects on economic occurrences.

Nat: (dubious) Stop right there. I admit I can't point to a single process that recurs repeatedly in all community spheres in the way that you pinpoint the accumulation process. But I can point to many social struggles where nationalist aspirations played primary roles. Or a combination of religion and nationalism. What about South Africa, Iran, China, India?

Marlen: Just a minute here. Racial and national dynamics operate to texture economic dynamics which alone set the stage for change.

Ana: Wait a second, Marlen. Even in the Soviet Union it was Lenin's party that played a central role in determining that change would be bureaucratic and statist, not socialist.

Marlen: But the state was not the basic motor for change.

Sofie: Hold the phone, Marlen. Your evidence only proves that economics is causally relevant, not that other spheres are irrelevant. I think we should look more closely at relations between gender and class. We could certainly find some laws of motion in that relationship which would help us understand historical change better than the continued assertion of economics alone as the basic motor for change.

Radfem: There's no question in my mind that the motor force in history is the striving of men for power over women.

Marlen: That kind of blindness simply proves my point. What evidence can you possibly have for that statement? The Russian Revolution? What kinship laws of motion occurred there? Don't make me laugh.

Coho: You each make the other laugh at your respective monist claims. I think, Marlen, that your point can never be proven. What evidence do you have of a revolution brought about by the forces of production bursting social relations of production? Your formula hasn't been verified anywhere, any time. Where is your evidence that in China or Cuba, for example, growing forces of production running up against constraining social relations caused their revolutions?

Marlen: I might say the same to you, Coho. Where are the laws of motion in Cohoism?

Coho: I repeat, Marlen, in what revolution have fettering forces brought about revolutionary change? (pause) All right, you don't or can't answer that one, let me try another. Let's suppose that growing forces encountering frozen relations could become important. What if what you say were true for developed capitalism: that there exist intrinsic economic dynamics which push developed capitalist economies inexorably toward revolutionary upheaval. Why are we then to deduce that only economics can move societies with capitalist economies? Or that only changes in economics could bring about other liberatory social structures?

Marlen: I repeat, Coho, you take your holism so far that nothing precise remains.

Coho: But I don't claim to know precise laws of history. Indeed, there are no precise, always operative laws in the sense you mean. We can say interesting things about how the four spheres will interact no matter what specific contours they may have. We can know what general kinds of conditions are impossible between spheres or inside spheres. We can discover that all societies of a particular type will always embody certain traits. But we can't say, for example, that every society will inevitably undergo such and such a pattern of development, or even that every capitalist economy or patriarchal kinship sphere will always follow such and such a trajectory. Other spheres may interfere.

Marlen: Like I said, no laws of motion.

Coho: You may not like it that we can't enunciate universal laws, but postulating violated laws doesn't improve the situation.

Sofie: I can agree with that. Why enshrine inaccurate laws? Even if we analyze certain intrinsic characteristics of a particular type of economy or state, we can't say with certainty that those characteristics will always operate in real societies.

Marlen: But why must we believe that the best we can come up with is general assertions about accommodation and co-reproduction and nothing more?

C.C.: Because while we can analyze specific societies and determine what historical pressures and trajectories are operating in them, we can't do it for all time and for all societies.

Coho: I would go even further. I would say that any theory that treats history as if there is a built in, unchanging economic script is a theory that ignores that the rules of historical development are themselves historical.

Marlen: (in disbelief) Are you calling me a-historical?

C.C.: I think she is.

Nat: I like the way this discussion is going.

Sofie: So do I.

Ana: I wonder why.

Radfem: I'm not sure I do.

Plury: Fits in with my thinking.

Coho: (insisting on this point) In every field of study, scholars develop theories that operate on many different levels. They make general theories about the behavior of solids, liquids, and gasses. They make more specific theories about compounds in general. Or about particular compounds. Or about molecules in general, or specific molecules, or elements in general, or specific elements, or atoms in general, or specific atoms.

Radfem: Science again.

Coho: We can theorize about qualities of all languages, or of all languages of a specific type, or of a particular language, or about all structures of a particular type within a particular language.

C.C.: But history is at a higher level of complexity than chemistry, biology, or linguistics. History involves all those things as well as living organs, thinking beings, elaborate networks of institutions and ideologies.

Coho: Still, the analogy can work. When we theorize general classes of things like all compounds or all languages we only discover broad possibilities and make predictions about ranges of possible outcomes. When we need more detail, for more precise results, we lower the level of abstraction and discuss particular compounds or languages. Then we discover more exacting rules which allow us to predict with greater precision and detail. And the same is true for societies and history.

Sofie: I see what you mean. We can theorize about societies and history in general or we can look at specific societies like the U.S. We would name the basic spheres in society economic, kinship, community, and political and we would use these spheres to theorize about society in general and about specific events that happen in society—about evolutionary and revolutionary patterns as they emerge in both particular societies and whole epochs.

Nat: For example, looking at the community sphere, we can talk about religion in general, catholicism in general, the catholic church, the church in Nicaragua, a particular parish, and so on.

Marlen: (unimpressed) You want me to believe that in the U.S., the Soviet Union, China, Cuba, or any other country, there are non-economic dynamics that significantly affect evolution and the prospects for revolution? Where is your evidence?

Coho: There is probably no evidence that will convince you. If I state that the formation of the working class in England was differentiated along gender lines because sexism produced in the kinship sphere caused both male workers and male capitalists to struggle to embody the same relations in the economy, partly to defend gender privilege as well as partly to use gender hierarchies to support class hierarchies, you would probably reply that no, gender divisions were produced only to divide the working class and had purely economic roots. If I describe the Soviet Union as a society that from birth was a social formation with a dictatorial bureaucratic state, a technocratic economic structure, an initially fragmented community sphere fraught with racism and pushed toward homogenization, and a kinship sphere with the nature of sexism altered but patriarchy intact, you would disagree. You see the Soviet Union as a society that had a socialist revolution in the economy, that was pressured by capitalist encirclement, illiteracy, and poverty: i.e. neither capitalist nor socialist, but coordinator, and I would highlight the other spheres as well.

We have such different pictures of things, Marlen, that I think you will never accept my evidence. But for all your "weight of history" and the past predominance of your well-developed economic theory, can you even explain struggles among coordinators, coordinators and workers, coordinators and central party bureaucrats over planning and markets in the Soviet system?

Nat: When, Marlen, have you ever adequately explained religious and cultural persecution or the positive dimensions of spirituality and power of cultural identifications?

Sofie: The limited access of women to positions of political influence?

Radfem: The distortion of sexual potentials?

Ana: Stalinism?

Coho: The question of what constitutes sufficient evidence to justify giving up an established widely-held perspective is difficult. Is the experience of the Soviet Union evidence enough? What if that experience combined with our theory of the coordinator class can counter any marxist claim that Leninism serves the working class? I think we have a plausible workable conceptual alternative. I think complementary holism gives us concepts that help understand things that marxism ignores. But not only that. They help us know that these are important areas of consideration in the first place. Complementary holism aims to give a generalized theory of the operations of history that will help us delimit the ranges of historical outcomes. It makes it possible to theorize certain types of institutions—economies or markets; communities, colonialism or specific cultures; states or parliaments; kinship or nuclear families—to then make predictions about general and more specific social dynamics. And it can help us theorize about trajectories of development, how spheres interact and change, and about force fields that radiate throughout society. Isn't that enough to warrant giving it a practical chance?

Marlen: I'm not giving up. Your methods give no priorities, no guidelines of focus. Going back to our early and ever-popular stew analogy, you've got a lot of vegetables, meat and potatoes floating around in a gravy with no way to decide which gives the stew its main flavor, which to eat first, what to add later. My concepts allow me to enjoy the stew even though clearly the dominant flavor comes from beef if it is a beef stew, lamb if it is a lamb stew, etc.

Sofie: I will never understand, Marlen why you cannot criticize your own theory. You argue for a set of laws of motion of some abstracted part of society which you then say will tell us all the important things we need to know about all of society.

Plury: I think, Marlen, you have made a strong case for the rest of us to simply get rid of the marxist framework.

Radfem: I agree. Talk about fetters.

Neopop: No problem for me. I left marxism behind some time ago. Marxist class analysis has become a handicap to a movement for social change. Class analysis, any kind of group analysis, promotes dissension and tension.

Coho: Now hold on. It is one thing to note that some of marxism's central concepts are flawed. But why overreact and reject all the insights marxism provides? That is going much too far. We need to improve marxism and incorporate its positive lessons, not reject it whole hog.

Neopop: No. I think we need to reject it because we need to unite people, not fragment them. We need to respect differences and value all sides of polarities. There are many different kinds of work, so why not value them all? The same for cultures and kinship roles. All you're doing, Coho, is expanding the number of correct political lines people must argue over. While Marlen would only criticize us for having the wrong line on the economy, you would criticize us for having the wrong line on just about everything. Why not simply propose a liberatory program that opposes all important oppressions and invite everyone to support it?

Coho: The danger of complementary holism becoming just another batch of lines, as you point out, is real—although I have never claimed that people should think, act, or look alike. Quite the opposite. Perhaps you were dozing but, in any event, your solution to the dangers of sectarianism has tremendous problems which I think cannot be corrected.

Neopop: I might have known.

Coho: Let me put this to you as a hypothesis. One approach to the fourfold core characteristics in our society is to analyze them from the perspective of those who are oppressed along each axis and then propose alternative visions which are fully liberatory for all.

Another approach, however, starts with the supposition that what is needed is to eliminate certain specific ills so that a particular group, rather than all groups, might benefit. My claim is that whenever the group in this second approach is one of those at the bottom of the hierarchy of the oppressed, liberation will be impossible without pervasive liberatory changes in all spheres of social life. But if the group is not one of those at the bottom, but rather the coordinator class, then activists engaged in elevating this class to economic supremacy could choose a politically effective program conducive to that more limited end. And I claim that decades ago, the best choice for a champion of coordinator interests was marxism since marxism could deflect attention from coordinator aims even while it helped coordinators organize other sectors to join the coordinator defined project. But nowadays almost any sustained thinking about classes reveals coordinators as important historical participants, and so marxism, which highlights class analysis, no longer serves coordinator needs well as it once did. It leaves too much possibility of people noticing the role of coordinators—even as it tries to prevent this. A better ideological choice, in the eyes of some coordinators, is to adopt some kind of populism rejecting all class analysis in favor of "unity." Of course, the marxist infatuation with markets and central planning for allocation can be retained, though coordinators will also want to emphasize the value of parliamentary democracy—which, of course, benefits them most of all.

C.C.: It sounds to me like in current situations you put the economy first.

Radfem: I knew it.

Nat: I suspected it.

Coho: In analyzing the program of a specific class, yes. But only because I see an emerging political program serving the economic interests of coordinators, under the guise of a popular front.

Neopop: Who said anything about the economic interests of coordinators? I offer constructive criticism and you label me an obscurantist enemy.

Marlen: Join the club.

Coho: If what I said applies to you, then I plead guilty of labeling. Changing society is not the same as having a friendly chat. A great deal is at stake. But I think I was only suggesting the dangers of an approach which, for whatever reason, says that classes are no longer relevant historical actors. There are even some who now argue that because work is inevitably boring and regimented, we should give up revolutionizing it and simply diminish the number of hours we spend working while increasing the amount of leisure time. Oppressions in the economic sphere remain as they were—we just suffer them for a shorter period of time. This not only risks losing any chance of attaining liberation in the other codefined and coreproduced spheres, it ignores that work, freely undertaken, is a critical element of a fulfilling life.

Marlen: (sensing affirmation) So, you admit the need for working class leadership in struggles to change history.

Coho: Of course. because I see that history has a critical economic component. But our movements must also be led by those whose interests lie in the elimination of all forms of domination.

Sofie: You know, while I don't agree with Neopop's approach, I must say that I am getting nervous again. I can easily see where your concepts, Coho, can sound very plausible, flexible, and inclusive. Everyone understands and is sensitive to everyone else. But what if the person or group of people using the theory are black people whose experiences differ from each other but who locate themselves in the community sphere. What makes them sensitive to the other spheres? Because they've studied and understood the theory? Maybe. But they haven't understood the experience of white women or women in the garment industry.

Nat: And the same would hold true for white women in the kinship sphere. What increases their sensitivity to community? They don't live where I do or suffer in the same way. Why would they incorporate the principles of co-definition and co-reproduction in a way I would applaud?

Radfem: What would make those concerned with sexual preference issues incorporate experiences of black auto workers, and vice versa?

Ana: What would make those addressing state power feel that any changes in that sphere were co-dependent on other spheres...

Plury: It just seems so impossibly complicated.

Coho: It's true that it requires a great deal. But we are talking about changing society. We can spend our energy branding people with simplistic labels and manipulating people's words and programs in sectarian ways or we can listen critically to familiar approaches, decide that they are less desirable than they might be, and openly and carefully develop new and better beliefs and goals.

Ana: Back off. You've already convinced me.

Nat: I don't know.

Radfem: If I thought men would actually...

Sofie: I'm getting there.

Coho: Shall I tell you about my thoughts on vision and strategy for a liberatory society?

Nat: Why not.

Cyn: (smugly) A liberatory society? That ought to be good.

(Coho rustles through her papers as the others wait eagerly)

Dialogue #8: Following Chapter Nine, "Strategy"

"Is There Some Way We Can Replace
This Dumb Label, 'Complementary Holism'?"

(Coho has just finished describing her thoughts on vision and strategy. As the others are busy making notes, gathering their own thoughts together, Cyn takes the momentary lull as an opportunity to set Coho straight on the question of human nature)

Cyn: (rising to stand near the window) No one regrets more than I having to say these things. My entire life has been wrapped up in social change. For years I've read, written, and organized in the area of international relations. I've seen radicals become fascists; I've seen comrades become apolitical bourgeois intellectuals; I've participated in meetings and events where the internal debates destroyed the spirit of almost all the participants. I appreciate your efforts, Coho, particularly your sketching of such comprehensive guidelines for developing visions of a new society. But I had visions once too. So did many others. I believed fervently in the possibility of a liberating society. I fought for it. Now I look at countries I supported, like China, and it just seems hopeless.

Coho: But the Chinese never created a humanist society, or even just a socialist economy.

Cyn: But they tried.

Coho: So did the Russians. You don't seem as bothered by their failures.

Cyn: So I'm a slow learner.

Coho: Perhaps. Or perhaps you were able to see that the Leninist failures were no more proof of the impossibility of a liberatory society than was the failure to create one in the U.S. after our revolution. Or in France after theirs.

Cyn: The U.S. revolution wasn't aimed at creating socialism.

Coho: The Russian revolution wasn't aimed at creating socialist economic relations or humanist relations in all four social spheres. It sought an authoritarian state, a coordinator economy, a homogenized community sphere, and a patriarchal kinship sphere. The leaders, at least, got what they sought. So did the leaders in China.

Cyn: That's nonsense. Soviet activists believed in a better world as much as we do. They gave their lives trying to win it.

Coho: Of course, I don't deny the integrity of the activists. They did desire equity, but their leaders actually instituted social forms which had contrary implications.

Cyn: Maybe there was no alternative. In China the Maoists certainly sought democracy.

Coho: Perhaps, in the end, but for too many years they used centrist organizations which reproduced domination relations. Their challenges to sexism, state authoritarianism, and class oppression were minimal. Their myopic cultural politics corrupted their community life as well as their attempts at democracy.

Cyn: That's not entirely true. During the years after the revolution many struggled to understand and create alternatives to coordinator dominance. But they failed...

Marlen: You wear your pessimism like a crown of thorns. Look at what existed in China before their revolution—starvation, violence, degradation, deprivation. Their achievements were immense, unparalleled in history...

Nat: And what about Cuba? Some of the African nations? There have been profound changes that have improved the quality of life in countries around the world. And in the U.S. too.

Coho: In any event, why should the failure of the Chinese and other revolutions to meet goals they never intended to meet, goals that we think they should have met, dissuade us from the possibility of a revolution that creates what we want?

Cyn: In spite of what you say, it still seems that no matter what we do, we will never get what we want. The final outcome is always corrupted. Either human nature insures that some will always rule and others obey, or unknown forces preserve domination even though they let us alter the forms that domination will take.

Coho: So your hypothesis is that people are innately evil in ways that preclude creating a humane society?

Cyn: It makes sense to me that explanations to our problems may lie with human nature.

Nat: Is it Darwin's theory that makes you believe that, or history?

Cyn: Both.

Coho: But there is nothing in biological understandings of how evolution contours organisms to suggest that a species would "wire in" a trait that runs counter to its own perpetuation. People might have capacities for aggression, since these could have been useful during our evolution. But it's hard to see why they would come to innately turn these aggressive tendencies against one another. It's infinitely more likely for evolution to have given us dispositions to seek to live peacefully in search of friendship, solidarity, continuity, assistance, and defense against other species. Greed against other species might make sense, but sociability within a species would be more conducive to genetic success than in-fighting.

Sofie: But even Coho talks of the survival of the fittest.

Ana: True. But survival of the fittest doesn't mean everyone kills off everyone else. In fact, it usually insures that within a species there will be a disposition toward mutual aid. An appeal to evolution doesn't give us evidence for a genetically evil human nature.

Cyn: Then look at the evidence from history.

Coho: Yes, if we assume innately evil people, we can certainly explain Hitler. We can explain exploitation, concentration camps, lynching, slavery, rape, and saturation bombing. But can we explain the good that people do?

Cyn: Circumstances sometimes stifle our anti-social inclinations or even cause our greed to produce sharing.

Coho: So people do good things because institutions and environments select sociability over innate greed? From what we have said about society's institutions they would be more likely to exaggerate our dispositions to...

Nat: Burn.

Marlen: Loot.

Radfem: Rape.

Ana: Rule.

Coho: I think your innate anti-social genes thesis makes it very difficult—almost impossible—to see why there is any good at all in the world. Your view of human nature leads to a world of unrestrained evil.

Cyn: But if people are instead innately social, inquisitive and creative, as you hypothesize, then how do you explain exploitation, genocide, race hatred, imperialism.

Coho: That's what theories of history reveal by showing that what happens throughout history depends on interrelations between "innately good people," complex environments, and social institutions. Evil is not inevitable in all times and places. It is produced and can be replaced.

Cyn: Suppose I could accept your argument that there is no compelling evidence for believing that human beings are basically so anti-social that a humane society is biologically impossible, it still wouldn't increase my hopes. Dominating ways are so entrenched that every effort to eradicate them only transforms them into new forms.

Plury: It's sad, Cyn, that your belief in the inevitability of injustice has become such a bedrock faith, almost part of your personality.

Cyn: Perhaps your optimism is just blind faith, and my pessimism is based on reality.

Coho: No. I think many people are cynical about human nature or social possibilities because a cynical viewpoint serves them well, not because they have lots of good arguments and evidence on their side.

Cyn: But there is historical evidence in favor of the view that we can't create a good society. No one ever has. And now maybe we've been on the wrong road too long to get off.

Coho: People said we couldn't fly, but now they take it for granted. But you are right that no one can prove we can win a better world short of doing it, but I have good arguments for why it hasn't been done yet that can give us hope. The fact that you don't want to hear them, that you choose a pessimistic option, is a rationalization.

Cyn: For what? I'm miserable this way.

Coho: People who believe in a better way of life know that the way we live now is criminal. Denial of freedoms, death by starvation and exploitation, denigration of people's capabilities are everywhere. If you see that these outcomes are socially produced, then you understand that every person who dies as a result was effectively murdered. Once you accept the possibility of attaining a humanist alternative, you have to be a terrible hypocrite, coward or cynic to live passively with the contrast between what is and what could be.

Cyn: I don't get the point of this.

Coho: If you only know enough to think that people are evil, or if you convince yourself of that no matter the contrary evidence at your disposal, then these daily murders are horrible but inevitable. You have no responsibility, no complicity.

Cyn: So we should all sing the Internationale and believe in the goodness of human nature triumphing over evil? That's so pathetic.

Coho: I'm not suggesting it. It isn't that people should leap to believe in the goodness of human nature. It would be masochistic for people to wallow in guilt over complicity in crimes against humanity unless you felt you could do something about it. If you don't see any way forward, then as a strategy for getting by it is probably most sensible to interpret the injustices as the flip side of progress and make the best of things.

Sofie: I know people who will be moved to tears by the profound humanity of certain characters in novels, or movies, or by people in history, even people they know. Then they'll read about some atrocity and proceed to denigrate all humanity as greedy monsters.

Coho: Illogical but not crazy.

Cyn: But that's not me. I've actively supported movements for social change. I want to act but I can't anymore. I don't think we can succeed.

Coho: But why rationalize this inability by calling people innately evil or by appealing to inevitability?

Cyn: You tell me.

Coho: Well, some people rationalize wanting to operate in mainstream society—to make money, or whatever—by denying the efficacy of being radical. Ordinarily the one-time leftist turning to journalism, or running for office, or otherwise trying to be comfortable in the midst of humanity's crimes will denigrate her or his past as utopian childishness. Trying to make it in society is rationalized as a new found maturity about what's possible.

Cyn: Once again, that's not me. I have no desire to work in mainstream society to prove that I am a mature person.

Plury: But you argue that it proves you are a realistic person.

Cyn: Yes, because it does.

Coho: Perhaps, but maybe there is something about the tasks required to be effective activists that you don't want to admit are needed. Or that you don't want to do.

Cyn: Perhaps I don't want to spend my time on earth in a losing battle, constantly looking at pain and suffering that I cannot put a stop to.

Coho: First, as a feeling person who has had the opportunity to learn what is really going on, can you find sustenance in maintaining injustice and degradation, or in looking the other way? Would you have felt better watching the Vietnam War on the six o'clock news? Could you have said to yourself, "since I can't know positively that any action I take will stop the war, I won't act at all even though I know how evil it is?" Or "since evil will always dominate, why bother? There will be another war, and another and another." After all, no group of people in the U.S. had ever previously stopped the government from waging a war it wanted to wage. It seems to me that even if the odds were against stopping the Vietnam War, that it was better to take a shot at it, than give up. But, second, we did help end the war. You did have an impact. And there is no compelling reason to think we can't have an effect again and again, not only on individual horrible policies, but once the great mass of people are involved, also on their underlying causes.

Cyn: Abstractly, I suppose I can agree that maybe the roots of my cynicism lies in rationalization rather than hard evidence. But that still doesn't make me want to rush back to the barricades...In fact, I feel paralyzed into inaction, pained and depressed by both choices.

Coho: But opposing oppression doesn't have to mean a lifetime of suffering. How can we persuade others to work for a better world if we live lives of pain and suffering, isolation and boredom. We don't have to ignore culture, music, personal relationships, food, beauty, humor, and sports, even interesting work. In fact, involvement, community, purpose, and a sense of humor can enhance our abilities immeasurably.

Neopop: (who finds Cyn a lost cause and has had enough) Speaking of abilities, and while I appreciate your efforts to lift Cyn's spirits, I really do have to get back to my work at which I am indispensible.

Marlen: (eager to discuss Coho's presentations on vision and strategy) Speaking of interesting work, your discussion of participatory planning raises many points which I would like to discuss at length.

Radfem: (rustling through papers to find visions chapter) Speaking of personal relationships, your notion of extended families could be enhanced if we...

Nat: (waving papers) Speaking of art, I was impressed by your arguments for diversity, although your hopes for...

Sofie: (arranging charts on the floor) While I would like to consign your notion of fields of force to the dustbin of a Hollywood Star Wars cutting room, I do like this business about codefinition and coreproduction. We should apply it even more generally...

C.C.: (rising and stretching) I think this economy vision with the concept of equitable job complexes is very good. But how...

Radfem: (rereading the kinship visions section) On the question of sexuality, you clearly aren't familiar with issues of erotophobia which...

Nat: (on the edge of his seat) When it comes to religion, you have a way to go. Clearly you've never had a religious day in your life. But if we elaborate...

Marlen: (taking a few volumes out of the bag he happened to bring along) Mind you, Coho, I don't agree with your methods but I think I could assist you in enriching your analysis to provide a deeper and more comprehensive vision...

Sofie: (frowning) This label complementary holism? It's all wrong. It's...

Nat: White.

Radfem: Male.

Marlen: Middle class.

Ana: Religious-sounding.

Plury: A mouthful.

Neopop: Inefficient.

C.C.: Strange.

Sofie: Dumb.

(Comments are beginning to fly fast and furiously as the group gets involved in the vision and strategy sections. Then a familiar voice from the corner quiets them down.)

Cyn: (tentatively, still holding on to the cloak of cynicism that has become a security blanket) Excuse me. I just wanted to say, without being too negative, that this vision chapter is somewhat naive and utopian. While I had been planning to leave for an appointment, I could stay a few minutes more to help provide a more realistic look at the possibilities...

Ana: Minutes? This is going to take longer than that. I have quite a bit to contribute to Coho's limited vision around hierarchies and decentralizing political forms which she obviously has little experience in...

Cyn: (on the verge of sliding back into the depths) I guess I could stay another hour.

Sofie: (only beginning her critique) Hours? We're talking about days.

Nat: Weeks.

Radfem: Months.

Cyn: (aghast) Months?

Plury: A year maybe.

Nat: In fact, we need another book. This one is too long already.

Cyn: (getting frantic) Another book?

Sofie: As a matter of fact, I have a few friends who would enjoy participating in further discussions of vision and particularly strategy and who could provide insights into the kinship arrangements...

Radfem: Since I am outnumbered around questions of sexuality, i know some people who could enlighten the discussion around...

Cyn: (worried) More people?

Nat: Exactly my thoughts with regards to racism and the discussion of the community...

Ana: My thinking also around hierarchies...I know some people who could really assist in the...

Cyn: (fighting off a returning cynicism) More people? Are you kidding? I can see it now, a hundred people in this room all arguing...

Sofie: Not a hundred. More like twenty-five.

Cyn: Well, I...

Marlen: (eager to get on with it) Now that we've agreed that we need more people and another book, and let me say I can contribute in that department, I want to say a few words, Coho, in our remaining time together, about the reductive nature of your strategy discussion where you equate strategies for economic revolution with a game of tic tac toe.

C.C.: Well said, Marlen. I really must object to the notion of strategizing a working class revolution around a chess board.

Plury: And basketball? Am I supposed to organize my people into sports leagues and then explain how each offensive play is really a plan for revolution? It's so...

Ana: Opportunist. Not to mention the competitive win/lose mentality it suggests. I really want to discuss this entire notion of strategy as you've presented it, Coho.

Coho: (couldn't be happier) Glad to, Ana. Clearly this is a stumbling block for many of you. You are equating analogies with actual practice. Since I think strategy is extremely important, and I am hoping we can refine it in the next book you have been talking about, I do think that we need to understand what I am getting at in my sports/games analogy. If I may demonstrate...?

Cyn: (clinging to old habits) Demonstrate? Surely you don't expect us to play...

Coho: (drawing on a large pad of paper) Now as I said in my presentation, there are simple strategies (draws tic tac toe) and there are complex strategies (draws basketball play board) Now let's say that Nat, Radfem, and Sofie are the offense and Plury, Neopop, and Marlen are the defense...

(the group gathers around, clearing chairs and making notes on the backs of pages)

Coho: In a basketball strategy we are working with...

Nat: Yes, we got that part.

Radfem: Tie in the analogy with some actual political strategies, Coho.

Ana: Let's have examples.

Cyn: (still in the corner chair, speaking without conviction, almost as a question) This isn't going to work...

Coho: Oh, but it is.

(We continue on with the discussion and we anticipate many more as our arguments develop and Coho's strategy board becomes increasingly complex.)

NOTES

Chapter One: Methods

1. Shulamith Firestone, *The Dialectics of Sex*, New York, Morrow, 1970.
2. David Bohm, *Wholeness and the Implicate Order*, London, Routledge and Kegan Paul, 1980.
3. Ilya Prigogine, *From Being to Becoming*, New York, W.H. Freeman, 1980 and *Order Out of Chaos*, with Isabelle Stengers, New York, Bantam, 1984.
4. Adrienne Rich, *Of Woman Born*, New York, Norton, 1976.

Chapter Two: Community

1. Frantz Fanon, *The Wretched of the Earth*, New York, Grove Press, 1968.
2. Paulo Freire, *Pedogogy of the Oppressed*, New York, Herter and Herter, 1971.
3. Ibid.

Chapter Three: Kinship

1. Rich, op. cit.
2. Kate Millett, *Sexual Politics*, Garden City, Doubleday, 1970.
3. Nancy Chodorow, *The Reproduction of Mothering*, Berekeley, Univ. of California, 1978.
4. Dennis Altman, *The Homosexualization of America*, New York, St. Martins, 1985.

5. Cherrie Moraga, *Loving in the War Years*, Boston, South End Press, 1983.
6. Robin Morgan, *Going Too Far*, New York, Random House, 1977.
7. Firestone, op. cit.
8. Rich, op. cit.

Chapter Four: Economics
1. Nancy Hartsock, "Feminist Theory and the Development of Revolutionary Strategy," in Zillah Eisenstein, *Capitalist Patriarchy and the Case for Socialist Feminism*, New York, Monthly Review, 1979.
2. Sam Bowles and Herb Gintis, *Schooling in Capitalist America*, New York, Basic Books, 1976.
3. Herbert Marcuse, *An Essay On Liberation*, Boston, Beacon Press, 1969.
4. Andre Gorz, (Michel Bosquet), *Capitalism in Crisis and Every Day Life*, London, Harvester Press, 1977.

Chapter Five: Politics
1. There was some doubt among us about using the word "politics" and some preference for a term like "governance" as a name for this last sphere, since general usage applies the term "politics" to all manner of struggle for change. However, since complementary holism emphasizes that the emanations of each sphere pervade all sides of life—not only politics but also economics, gender, and kinship have universal impact—we decided to stay with the more revealing term to designate the sphere centered around the state.
2. E.E.Schattschneider, *The Semi-Sovereign People*, New York, 1960
3. Michael Crozier, Samuel P. Huntington, Joji Watanuki, *The Crisis of Democracy*, New York, New York University Press, 1975.
4. Ibid.

Chapter Six: Society
1. Murray Bookchin, *The Ecology of Freedom*, Palo Alto, Cheshire Books, 1980.

Chapter Seven: History

1. Frederick Engels, The Dialectics of Nature, Moscow, 1954.
2. Karl Marx, *Preface to the Introduction to the Critique of Political Economy, New York*, International Publishers.

About South End Press

South End Press is a nonprofit, collectively run book publisher with more than 200 titles in print. Since our founding in 1977, we have tried to meet the needs of readers who are exploring, or are already committed to, the politics of radical social change. Our goal is to publish books that encourage critical thinking and constructive action on the key political, cultural, social, economic, and ecological issues shaping life in the United States and in the world. In this way, we hope to give expression to a wide diversity of democratic social movements and to provide an alternative to the products of corporate publishing.

Through the Institute for Social and Cultural Change, South End Press works with other political media projects—Z Magazine; Speakout, a speakers' bureau; and Alternative Radio—to expand access to information and critical analysis.

To order books, please send a check or money order to: South End Press, 7 Brookline Street, #1, Cambridge, MA 02139-4146. To order by credit card, call 1-800-533-8478. Please include $3.50 for postage and handling for the first book and 50 cents for each additional book. Write or e-mail southend@southendpress.org for a free catalog, or visit our web site: http://www.southendpress.org.

Other titles of interest from South End Press:

Looking Forward:
Participatory Economics in the Twenty-first Century
Michael Albert and Robin Hahnel

Necessary Illusions:
Thought Control in Democratic Societies
Noam Chomsky

Washington's War on Nicaragua
Holly Sklar

Remaking Society:
Pathways to a Green Future
Murray Bookchin

Yearning:
Race, Gender and Cultural Politics
bell hooks

From the Ground Up:
Essays on Grassroots and Workplace Democracy
C. George Benello